Gardens in the *Spirit* of *Place*

Gardens in the

Stewart, Tabori & Chang   New York

Spirit of Place

PAGE DICKEY *Photography by* John M. Hall

Foreword by Wayne Winterrowd

CONTENTS

FOREWORD

When Page Dickey enters a garden, she presents the same enthusiasm she must have felt when, as a child, she made her own first garden out of pebbles and wildflowers in a secret clearing in the woods. Her enthusiasm and eager curiosity about how a garden was made and works have served her well in writing this book, and indeed, in her career as one of America's most important garden writers. All over North America, in places of varied manners and social styles, people have welcomed her, showed her their gardens, and then sent her on to their gardening friends with an assured introduction. Page's energy and personal charm gain her entry into places, sometimes quite private ones, where other garden writers and photographers have not ventured. We, her readers, are fortunate to tag along with her.

Page's gardening experience spans a period of almost forty years and is recorded in her meticulously kept journals as well as a number of books. Her journals reflect a lifetime of quiet, independent research and contain observations, newly gathered knowledge, and exquisite small drawings. Her books, beginning with *Duck Hill Journal* in 1991, all reveal shrewd, sensible, deeply informed knowledge and explore her belief that "our gardens can be eclectic visions of independent-minded gardeners, as varied as is our vast country." Her award-winning *Breaking Ground* highlighted the work of ten young American and European garden designers, while *Inside Out* examined the relationship between a house and its surrounding garden. For Page, a house without a garden, or a garden without a house, simply makes no sense.

It is no surprise that this book includes almost as much about houses and the way people live in them as the gardens they fashion to surround them. As Page writes, "The more I travel around our vast country, reveling

Garden designer Edwina von Gal creates visual tension by contrasting a swath of closely mown lawn against a field of softly swaying *Panicum,* or switch grass, in a garden on Long Island.

in our disparate landscapes, the more I delight in gardens—and the houses they surround—that are in harmony with their landscape, and celebrate their regionality...." Eighteen remarkable gardens are profiled in this book, and they are all "gardens in the spirit of the place." From Nantucket and Maine, to Virginia and Texas, to Los Angeles and the Northwest, Page celebrates gardens, and gardeners, with "a passionate, intimate involvement in the land."

Through the almost translucent medium of Page's words, we share in her vision. Any really good garden book must be thoroughly read to be fully understood. In the case of this one, there is no need to take notes, to dog-ear pages, to highlight in yellow or apply stickums. If you read quietly and for pure pleasure, you will come to understand a way of seeing that is crucial to the making of a successful garden.

John Hall's shimmering photographs, which so beautifully illuminate the subjects of this book, support this way of seeing. Particularly thrilling is the way he captures the structure of plants and great trees, and the way light falls on a garden. Houses are revealed in their quiet dignity or quirky eccentricity, and garden furniture becomes at once sculpture and a cozy invitation to sit and rest. Working together, Page and John "give to airy nothings/A local habitation and a name." But perhaps it is featured gardener Julie Speidel who best expresses the philosophy of this book, that all great gardens exist in a specific place and context, and "there's an honoring you have to do to the land."

—Wayne Winterrowd, North Hill, Readsboro, Vermont

INTRODUCTION

The more I travel around our vast country, reveling in our disparate landscapes, the more I delight in gardens—and the houses they surround—that are in harmony with their landscape and celebrate their regionality. These gardens are made with a sensitivity to the demands of the site, its climate, its soil, its topography, as well as a regard for the aesthetics of their surroundings. The vernacular architecture has been noted and sometimes echoed, the area's indigenous stone walls and fences referred to, its native trees, hills, fields, and woods respected. A sampling of these reflective gardens has been gathered for this book—gardens in the spirit of the place.

On a recent autumn trip to Santa Fe, New Mexico, where the Great Plains and the Chihuahuan Desert meet the mountains of the Colorado Plateau, I marveled at the dramatic beauty of the vast arid countryside. Sagebrush, asters, sunflowers, and chamisa flourished along sand-colored ridges dotted richly with pinyon pine and juniper. Within the walls of soft-edged adobe houses and around contemporary flat-roofed homes, I found gardens in sympathy with this landscape, where native yellow-flowered chamisa mingled with gray-leaved herbs, where penstemons, salvias, and agastaches colored the ground with pink and coral, and grasses were interwoven with Mexican hat and purple prairie clover. But to my astonishment, gardens of water-thirsty delphiniums, roses, and hostas surrounding emerald green lawns were even more prevalent. These were called "oasis gardens," probably made by transplanted Easterners, and indeed were just that—startlingly at odds with their mountain-desert-grassland context, and oblivious to Santa Fe's scarcity of water.

A garden can be wonderful as an isolated object, rather like a piece of jewelry in a box, contained behind walls or within hedges, or tucked in a

Stacked-rail zigzag fences typically mark Wisconsin farmland. At the Meyer homestead, rails snake along the farmhouse road in front of a planting of prairie dock, wild bergamot (*Monarda fistulosa*), and purple coneflowers (*Echinacea purpurea*).

city where there is no need for a connection with its surroundings. But the gardens I have chosen for this book are not insular works of art, divorced from what is around them. Rather, they are formed by their environments.

This is not a book for native-plant purists. Although trees, shrubs, and perennials indigenous to the site are an essential part of each design, native plants are not used exclusively in order to make these gardens connect to their landscape. Who in the Northeast, for instance, would forgo lilacs, peonies, and daffodils because they are not native? These well-loved plants of Europe and Asia have adapted comfortably to the growing conditions here, and have become part of the vernacular, perfectly at home ornamenting old farmhouses. In California, few would want to give up rosemary, santolina, Spanish lavender, or any plant native to the Mediterranean that looks so at home in this similar climate. The criteria for the plants chosen by the gardeners in this book are that they will thrive within the ecological limits of each environment without cosseting, that they are not invasive, and seem appropriate to their settings in habit and character.

What is characteristic of a place evolves with the passing of decades, or more profoundly, centuries. Northeastern meadows are dappled with ox-eye daisies, chicory, bouncing Bet, and Queen Anne's lace, all European natives brought here by the colonists. Some plants and bugs, innocently imported, have proved invasive and uncontrollable, dramatically and tragically changing the landscape. Sugar maples alone now line New England

ABOVE: Low stone retaining walls are used by Edwina von Gal to level the ground in a transformed potato field on Long Island.

OPPOSITE: Clipped balls of boxwood, a constant theme in Robert Jakob's cottage garden on the East End of Long Island, lead down paths that thread through old shrub roses, flowering perennials, and small ornamental trees. Native red cedars, *Juniperus virginiana,* provide a richly somber background.

streets and shade the houses where a century ago elms stood like tall vases. Some day the sugar maples might disappear, wiped out by another beetle or the thuglike Norway maple, which is seeding in the woods and crowding out the native flora. Even deer are gradually changing the character of the countryside. In the Eastern woodland, they browse away the native understory plants, leaving Japanese barberry and Oriental bittersweet to take over.

It is inevitable, as the world becomes smaller, that regional purity is lost in gardens. Some of the changes are accidental, but many are deliberate, for of course we want to grow plants from all over the world—it would be hard to resist the vast palette available to us. And it is undeniably fun to grow something unexpected, exotic. A tropical garden pulled off in summertime in New York or Vermont is a piece of theater. It dazzles and is exciting. But the sorts of gardens explored in this book offer something more lasting—a satisfying calmness achieved by plantings that blend with the natural landscape. Their very suitability is soothing to the eye.

If the color of the pebbles and types of stones peculiar to each surrounding area (granite, flint, red rock) are noted and echoed in the gravel paths and walls that bind our gardens, the result will further enhance this calm aesthetic. On the edge of New England where I live, the old, tumbled, lichen-covered farm walls of rounded granite rocks weave endlessly through the countryside. These walls, originally made to clear the pastures in the nineteenth century, set the tone of economy

Venerable live oaks set the stage for a powerfully dramatic garden and create dappled shade on the terraces at architect Ted Flato's home in San Antonio.

and unpretentiousness. In contrast, the slick, sharply cut, angular stone walls and pillars that grandly announce some of the newest houses here jar the eye.

Plants and hardscaping greatly affect the appropriateness of a garden, but the accompanying architecture also plays a major role. In many parts of America—except in the wealthiest enclaves, where fantasy rules—an indigenous style of building is noticeable, either in the repeated use of a material, or in details, or often in a historical reference. Think of weathered shingle in Nantucket and along the beachfronts of Long Island, Arts and Crafts-style bungalows in Colorado, fieldstone farmhouses in Pennsylvania, brick and fancy ironwork in South Carolina, smooth masonry in Arizona, walled courtyards redolent of the Spanish Missions in California. If we keep in mind this indigenous architecture where we live, and build our houses as well as the outbuildings, walls, and fences in their spirit, then they, too, will fit pleasingly in their surroundings.

Gertrude Jekyll, who championed her local village vernacular in her writings at the beginning of the twentieth century, lamented even then that "more than half the new houses one sees give some uncomfortable if not actually painful impression, as of some exiled exotic unwilling to be acclimatized." She urged her readers to preserve the character of the land upon which a house and its garden were built, and to "have a house that sits at home upon this ground." Miss Jekyll would have heartily approved of Frank Lloyd Wright, who spoke of his architectural masterpiece, Fallingwater, in Pennsylvania as a "response to a site."

All the gardeners profiled in this book—some professional designers, some passionate amateurs—have responded to their surroundings with simplicity, daring, and originality. The resulting gardens, whether in the Northwest, Wisconsin, Texas, or Maine, stem from an appreciation of where they live, rather than a yearning for somewhere else.

Sun-loving yellow- and blue-flowering perennials, such as yarrow, coreopsis, bachelor buttons, and flax, mingle with herbs and bulbs in Mary McConnell's kitchen garden in the Piedmont region of Virginia. Sorrell gone to seed provides a decorative vertical.

On Farmland

I've always loved the look of farmland. The sight of neat rows of vegetables gives me pleasure. I love the satisfying pattern of orchards, their strict geometry contrasting with the graceful branching of the fruit trees. I find charming the ridiculous scale of a towering vase-shaped elm or a row of massive maples shading a diminutive clapboard farmhouse. I love to see the twisted trunks of old lilacs by a barn door, or stiff rows of gladiolas in modest front yards. I thrill to the golden stripes formed by hay just cut, or hay bales rolled and resting like great pale sculptures on the stubbled ground. There is poetry in the simple formality of agricultural patterns, and a plainness, a homeliness that is appealing.

The farms are vanishing from the outskirts of our great cities as land values soar. Commuters now live in the old farmhouses, and new houses are built in the fallow pastures. Vestiges of the old agricultural way of life remain in the setting—in meadows parceled by tumble-down granite walls or stacked rail fencing, in the old barns and houses, in the great old trees that line the roads, and the ancient apple tree standing alone now in a field. Even so, builders pay no attention to this lingering vernacular. People bring their dreams of a home in styles that speak of other places—Tudor, Georgian, Palladian, Southern Plantation, with little regard for the pastoral setting. Developers who buy up abandoned farmland build communities of large, bland dwellings with a dull sameness throughout the East and Midwest. The houses, surrounded by lawns liberally peppered with conifers, in communities entered through important stone piers, are purposely, it seems, disconnected from their locality.

The owners of the three properties described in the following pages, in contrast, relate to their bucolic farm settings in a distinctive way. These very different houses and gardens are suited to their specific sites in the vanishing pastures of Wisconsin, the outskirts of New York City, and Long Island, but they all have in common a sympathy for the farmland's utilitarian simplicity, its patterns and modest air.

The rampant trumpet vine (*Campsis radicans*)
jubilantly eradicates a utility pole in Pewaukee, Wisconsin.

KEITH KROEGER

An Architect's Barnyard in New York State

Keith kroeger is an architect with a
love of barns. He loves the simplicity of their utilitarian shapes, the fact that they are invariably tall
and well proportioned, and that they tend to be set in groups, creating
courtyard-like spaces. He finds these simple block barn shapes ideal for
shaping into a contemporary home and garden and appropriate in the
gently rolling countryside of farms and fields where he lives just fifty
miles north of New York City. Second-growth woodland covers much
of this rock-strewn area now, around settlements of houses. But
miraculously, patches of open pastoral landscape survive this close to
the city. The wooden barns and the open fields, sectioned by dry-
stacked stone walls, are a legacy from the nineteenth century, when dairy
and sheep farmers cleared a large percentage of the natural oak woods
for pastures.

Until recently, Keith lived with his wife, Susan, in a converted
Victorian barn, reveling in its spaciousness and shaping a dramatic
garden of hedges and walls in its lea; but like most architects, he longed
to build his own home from scratch. With that in mind, the Kroegers
bought a four-acre parcel of fields and woods near an old horse farm on
a rural road, and for three years, Keith played with his barn shapes on
paper. Finally, they built their dream house based on those vernacular
barn structures.

English and Boston ivy soften
the stark outline of a free-
standing masonry wall. The
wall conceals one part of the
garden from another, adding a
sense of surprise.

Keith delights in the fact that from the
road you can't be sure the cluster of three gray-
brown barns with metal roofs is a home for
other than horses or cows. Almost no windows

Architect Keith Kroeger designed the studio and living quarters as separate barnlike structures and set them, as they often were traditionally, into a grass bank. Windows the size of barn doors in the studio and in Susan and Keith's living room afford spectacular views of the surrounding meadow and its wildlife.

are apparent, and the structures are pared down to their simplest shapes. Dry fieldstone walls enclose and shield the entrance drive and parking area, and along with hedges of tightly clipped forsythia, block views of an inner courtyard and garden. Beyond the barns is a glimpse of a meadow of high grass rimmed by a wood of maple and oak.

But once you've parked your car, and walked through the wooden farm gate between two of the barns, you are surprised to be standing in the first of a series of formally ordered outdoor garden rooms. Here, through a pattern of littleleaf lindens planted in gravel, Keith's elegantly windowed home is revealed. The largest of the three barns, L-shaped and two-stories high, contains Keith and Susan's living quarters. The undetailed windows in this house are oversize, like barn openings, framing views of the garden on two sides and the meadow and woods on the third as if they were paintings. A second barn, serving as Keith's studio, faces the living room of the house, and opens on two opposite sides with barnlike doors to reveal a vignette in the garden. The third barn, at right angles with the house and studio, serves as the garage, although it looks like it might just as well shelter cows or horses. The three barns, linked by walls and gates, define the boundaries of the garden.

Unlike the untamed woods and long grass that lap the outer walls of Keith and Susan's barn-house, the interior garden is dramatically structured, spare and formal, made with an architect's love of space defined by trees, walls, hedges, and columns. In the courtyard garden by the entrance

to his house, Keith planted five handsome linden trees. He chose the smaller-growing European form, *Tilia cordata*, rather than the massive native basswood, *Tilia americana*, which towers over old farmhouses in the neighborhood. The L-shape house and the garage form three sides of this graveled entrance garden; on the fourth side is a stuccoed, cement-block wall laced with vines.

Through a second gate, the courtyard leads into a small grassed garden, walled on all sides and punctuated by free-standing rectangular columns of stucco, painted the same sand color as the walls and stucco chimney of the house. These columns, decorated only with tendrils of vines, give structure to the space, making it seem larger than it is. They also define the boundaries of a lap pool and loggia set in the grass. Some carry wooden crosspieces, which will eventually be softened with the vines; others stand alone, reminiscent of a ruin, Keith says.

Glimpsed from the road, the Kroegers' home might be mistaken for a typical local horse or cow farm; what appear to be metal-roofed barns give no hint of the home and garden's elegance evident within the farm gate. On top of the stone wall that lines the entrance drive, Keith planted masses of the ubiquitous forsythia, which he clips hard to achieve a sculptural shape.

On axis with the pool, an opening in the far wall leads to the final room of the formal garden: a narrow stretch of lawn planted with a row of crab apple trees—Keith's homage to the apple orchards that were once abundant in this area. Behind the impeccably pruned crabs, a high stuccoed wall, partially covered with a tracery of ivies and Virginia creeper, marks the side of the property line. Past the line of fruit trees, a farm gate in a dry fieldstone wall opens onto a soft, waving field of meadow grass. Although the width of the lot—two hundred feet—where Keith has set his barns and garden is narrow by country standards, in length the four-acre property extends generously into meadow and wood.

As much as Keith loves the small architectural garden he has created within the confines of his three barns, he and Susan are rapturous about the field they have nurtured beyond their house and the wildlife this natural landscape brings to their windows. When houses are being built, the character of the land surrounding the building site is inevitably destroyed. In Keith's case, he was able to save several mature oaks and maples and a glorious large Eastern red cedar (*Juniperus virginiana*) when they cleared for construction. But in terracing the land

so that the barn-house would sit comfortably into the sloping ground, he was left with a sea of weeds where there once was meadow. Keith used Roundup to kill the weeds, then slit-sowed the land with a seed mixture of native grasses. Mulched by the debris of dead weeds, the grasses flourished, restoring the soft natural look of the field. Keith and Susan thrill to its changing character. "I love the grass all long and growing," Keith says, "but one of the great hands-on pleasures is then to mow it," which usually happens in September. The smell, he says, is fabulous, and he delights in the changing textures of the grid pattern left by the mowing machine going one way and then another.

What the new meadow also affords is a natural habitat. Outside the great windows passes a parade of wildlife. Deer, of course, linger here

OPPOSITE, TOP AND BOTTOM: A secret, formally structured garden lies within the confines of the buildings and connecting walls; outside them the natural landscape is preserved. A simple lap pool, set in lawn, is furnished with stuccoed concrete columns.

ABOVE: "There's nothing I like better than the classic outdoor room," Keith says. In autumn, Boston ivy (*Parthenocissus tricuspidata*) and Virginia creeper (*P. quinquefolia*) redden the walls and columns in this architectural garden.

ABOVE: In the raked-gravel courtyard surrounded by the L-shape house and garage, Keith planted a pattern of littleleaf linden trees (*Tilia cordata*) and positioned two terra-cotta jars in their shade.

OPPOSITE: Barns tend to have large sliding doors opposite each other, which, when open, draw the eye through the interior to a distant perspective. This characteristic inspired Keith's design of the studio, where an urn is placed inside on axis with a crab apple tree beyond.

(they avoid the garden because of the solid walls), and flocks of turkeys are often spotted. On a recent Thanksgiving Day, Susan and Keith watched a red fox sunning himself in the meadow. Coyotes frequently lope by. A snapping turtle appears every June to lay her eggs. "We have bluebirds galore," Susan says. In fact, the meadow, which is set on the edge of a wet woodland, is ideal for birds. "It's a soaring place," she says. Plans are afoot for a winter garden that would feed the birds and paint a haze of color along the wet wooded edge of the field: native winterberries glowing scarlet in November and December; shrub dogwoods, like *Cornus racemosa*, with chalk-white fruit on crimson calyces; perhaps a sweep of cranberry bush viburnums.

Keith considers himself a minimalist in gardening as well as in architecture; he prefers repeating one element (or massing one sort of plant) and limiting his palette for a powerful effect. The sculpted blocks of forsythia at the driveway entrance are a case in point—Keith enjoys using this common, overused plant in an unusual way by massing it in tight clusters and clipping it into dramatic cloudlike hedges. The punch of yellow in April is almost neon against the tree-bark color of the barns. In summer and fall, the mounded hedges are satisfying green architecture; in winter, their warm brown twigwork, Keith notes, is pleasurable too, and moreover, is home to cardinals. Vines are a repeated theme, trained on the house chimney, walls, and garden columns. Keith uses Boston ivy as well as the hardy English ivy called '238th Street' to climb the stucco surfaces, and interweaves them with Virginia creeper and the occasional climbing hydrangea. "I like planting them all together and letting them duke it out," he says. He loves the patterns they create on the walls, and how

their leaves turn color with the changing seasons. An added bonus is that birds nest in the vines.

Very few flowers are used in the garden besides a series of Italian clay pots filled in summertime with red geraniums. Although Keith admits he is tempted by flowers, there's the issue of time. Because he likes to do his own gardening—the watering, pruning, fertilizing, fussing—and at the same time has an active architecture practice, there is a certain logic to the minimal approach. "Left to my own devices," he adds, "I like things that are really simple. The less-is-more school."

The striking simplicity of Keith's home and garden is what makes it remarkable. Jens Jensen, the great early twentieth-century landscape architect from the Midwest, listed qualities he found essential in a garden—among them, a sense of place, coherence, complexity, and mystery. Keith achieves coherence in the simple repetitive nature of his design. The complexity of his garden with its patterns of trees, walls, and vines is hidden until you are within its walls. Here, then, is the mystery and the pleasure of surprise. But the suitability of the house and garden are immediately apparent. They sit comfortably on the land, and together with the restored meadow and surrounding trees speak of the place.

Wisconsin Homestead

MUCH OF THE MIDWEST CAN APPEAR TO be an endless expanse of farmland—a paper-flat pattern of cultivated land laid out in perfect circles and rectangles of green and gold. But in the Midwest's northern reaches, three distinctly native features define the landscape as well: oak-hickory woodland, a network of lakes, and remnants of prairie. By the early twentieth century, almost all the virgin tallgrass prairie that covered the southern half of Wisconsin and Minnesota and most of Illinois (as well as Iowa, Nebraska, Kansas, and Oklahoma) had disappeared under the plow, replaced by rich farmland of corn, wheat, and soybean. In the last ten years, however, pioneering native plantsmen, like Wisconsin's Neil Dibble, Laurie Otto, and Darrell Morrison, have opened our eyes to the wealth and beauty of what Walt Whitman considered to be America's most characteristic landscape. A new, nationwide reverence for the prairie's brilliantly colored, drought-tolerant, winter-hardy, butterfly-attracting summer flowers, as well as a growing appreciation of self-sustaining native plant communities, have resulted in restored and replanted patches of this unique habitat. Purple coneflower and sunflowers wave in small Midwestern backyards and fields of big blue stem and liatris flourish along the roadsides. More important perhaps, vast preserves of prairie now exist thanks to the efforts of organizations like the Nature Conservancy, the Chicago Botanic Garden, and the Arboretum at the University of Wisconsin.

The old farmhouse in Pewaukee, Wisconsin, is virtually unchanged since the 1930s. A line of silver maples, planted then, now shade the house.

Fortunately, forests of oak and hickory continue to surround farmland and lakes in much of Wisconsin, Minnesota, Michigan, and

Old-fashioned single-flowering hollyhocks tower against the old barn in July. A brace of bamboo stakes, lashed together, hold them upright.

Illinois, where developments of suburban sprawl have not swept away all signs of the natural landscape. Majestic oaks still shade suburban streets and tower over country gardens on the outskirts of cities like Chicago, Milwaukee, and Detroit. The oceanlike Great Lakes also give a singular character to this part of our country, as does the lacework of smaller lakes that make Wisconsin and Minnesota, in particular, look on a map like so much Swiss cheese.

Tony Meyer, a child psychiatrist, and his wife, Donna, have raised their three children on a property that combines all the features that distinguish the landscape of Wisconsin. They live on forty acres of farmland and oak woods that rise above Lake Pewaukee, one of fifteen thousand lakes that glitter across this Midwestern state. In the nineteenth century, Tony's great-grandparents traveled from Milwaukee to this nearby bucolic place by train and buggy to spend weekends and summer vacations by the water's edge. They bought woodland that bordered the lake, and, on higher ground, land that was cleared for farms. It was here that

subsequent generations of Tony's family put down roots and where Tony spent his childhood.

A collection of wooden masks serves as scarecrows in Tony Meyer's vegetable garden behind the farmhouse.

The property that Tony and Donna have called home since the 1960s, down the lake from the Meyers' original homestead, was a pig farm in the early years of the twentieth century. The pigs were pastured in the cleared fields around the small farmhouse and the stone-and-clapboard barn; in fall they foraged for hickory nuts and acorns in the woods. In the 1930s, on the day Tony was born, his grandfather purchased this additional forty-acre farm and used it to raise sheep. When Tony was a boy, the cleared land—about ten acres—around the old farmhouse was planted entirely with sunflowers. It was a sea of sunflowers in summer, Tony recalls, and "the whole field would turn and follow the sun." Tony remembers his grandfather driving an old car through the fields in spring, tossing out sunflower seed as he went, while his grandmother fretted that he would get stuck in the mud. "For a time my father raised mink here," Tony says, remembering his father's interest in animal husbandry and a

Twig supports in Donna Meyer's farmyard flower garden guide scarlet cardinal vines in front of a token row of sunflowers.

fascination with genetics, breeding for different-colored coats. Eventually the farm went to his maiden aunt, and then finally to him.

Animals no longer fill the barn at the Meyers', and only a token row or two of sunflowers nod above the beds of cottage flowers in Donna's farmyard garden. But the spirit of the farm remains intact. An old red tractor, idle now, rests by the vegetable garden, and the farmhouse and barn remain unchanged since their early days. The barn, long and low, its wooden clapboards typically stained red over a fieldstone base, houses the old farm truck, and, in early summer, a family of barn swallows nests in the crook of a watering can hanging from a beam. Hollyhocks—the old-fashioned single sorts—in hues of pink, red, yellow, apricot, and cream, crowd against the sheltered south side of the barn, flowering all of July and into August. Across the dirt drive that runs in front of the barn and ends at the farmhouse, Donna planted a small field of prairie flowers; they were grown from seed that she and her son Nick gathered from the verges of the Milwaukee Road railroad nearby. Sawtooth sunflowers, gray coneflowers (*Ratidiba pinnata*), prairie dock (*Silphium*), and elmleaf goldenrod flower among big blue stem grasses here in August and September.

Clay pots of coral pink geraniums, stored in the cellar every winter and brought back to life each spring with a swig of fertilizer, line the brick walk from the drive to the farmhouse porch in summer. Here, a porch swing and chairs painted turquoise and coral are favored places to sit with a cool drink. A row of venerable silver maples, planted by Tony Meyer's grandfather, arch over and dwarf the small two-story house. Beds of lilies-of-the-valley and white hydrangeas simply and appropriately border its foundation. Beyond the stand of maples is Donna's fenced-in flower garden where, until the late 1950s, stood nothing but sunflowers. Later on, a cutting garden and orchard were planted there by Tony's Aunt Margaret.

Coral pink geraniums are kept from year to year to line the walk to the farmhouse. They are stored in the dark cellar in winter, then brought to life with a swig of fertilizer in spring.

The orchard remains. In front of it, Donna has filled the fifty-by-seventy-five-foot garden with a merry mixture of annuals, perennials and bulbs that stand up to the Midwestern heat—snapdragons, zinnias, lilies and alliums, balloon flowers (*Platycodon*), mallows, dancing meadow rues and anthericums, nasturtiums, and aconites. Sunflowers have a bed of their own, and pink everblooming roses are clustered in another bed. This year, a row of asparagus and another of raspberries were relegated to the vegetable garden behind the barn and replaced with orange dahlias. "I love the combination of orange and pink," Donna admits, "Gina Lollobrigida pink." Scarlet cardinal vines twine around tall supports that have nestlike balls fashioned out of grapevines on top. Balls are a playful theme, and reappear on the surrounding fence, made with wire and farm posts that

ON FARMLAND

ABOVE: The beautiful late-blooming native prairie rose, *Rosa setigera*, fountains over the stacked-rail, zigzag fence along the farm road.

ABOVE RIGHT AND OPPOSITE: The Meyers turned wooden farm-posts upside down like pencils and topped them with wooden balls painted turquoise blue to mark the boundaries of the flower garden where balloon flowers (*Platycodon*) and globe thistles mingle with roses and nicotiana.

Tony and Donna sunk upside down like pencils jammed in the ground and topped with wooden spheres painted turquoise blue. This blue is another theme, its cue taken from small colored panes that surround the farmhouse windows. The color is repeated on painted screen doors as well as porch and garden furniture.

Although they delight in their flower garden, Donna is quick to say it is only one small part of the farm, a portion of the place they celebrate as home. A brimming vegetable garden decorated with Tony's collection of modern masks on posts (serving as scarecrows) is planted yearly behind the barn. Beyond it, paths are mowed through ten acres of meadow. The farmhouse itself shelters visiting children, grandchildren, and guests, and is a favorite place to have breakfast or even dinner in the summertime.

The Meyers' small lake house, a typical nineteenth-century Wisconsin summer house of porch windows and gables, is painted a cheerful combination of pale green, lavender, and white, and stands on stilts above a fieldstone foundation near the water's edge. It is inevitably bursting in summer with the two Meyer daughters, Eliza and Christina, and their

families and is a frequent destination for lunches and barbecues. The lake house is just a short distance down from the farm, through shadowy woodland and is planted simply with sweeps of mophead white hydrangeas and pagoda dogwoods. Its windows and terrace look out onto a broad lawn stretching down to the shore, the view framed by a line of towering oaks. A small float bobs in the water; it is made from a little sailboat, moored and filled in with fiberglass so it is flat. From its mast flies a fabric pennant painted with the face and streaming hair of Botticelli's *Venus,* that was made by Eliza.

Between the lake and the farm, in woods where the pigs rooted for acorns and hickory nuts eighty years ago, Donna and Tony have their winter home. It is a pleasant walk from the farmhouse along a dirt road, past stacked-rail zigzag fencing so typical of Wisconsin, behind which great clumps of prairie dock and lavender bee balm bloom in August and September. *Rosa setigera*—the beautiful prairie rose—fountains over the fence with clusters of single pale pink flowers in July. The road leads into the woods where ferns and waving white plumes of snakeroot take over

The Meyers' property slopes down to the shores of Lake Pewaukee where their nineteenth-century lake house is a preferred family destination in summer. Banks of mophead hydrangeas nestle here beneath pagoda dogwoods (*Cornus alternifolia*) and tall oaks.

from prairie flowers. This third shelter on the Meyer property, nestled in the shade of tall oaks, is contemporary architect David Kahler's take on the Wisconsin dairy barn, half of a barn actually, with silo, painted a playful yellow and blue-green. This is where Tony and Donna sleep year round, where they work (Tony's office is in the silo), and where they entertain in the chill of winter. Donna has kept the surrounds of the house simple, encouraging ferns and planting shrubs such as native dogwoods and viburnums that thrive in the understory of the oaks and hickories. A sculpture of an unfurling ostrich fern, which Nick created from interlocking pieces of wood, rises out of the sea of ferns by the back terrace.

No one in the Meyer family farms anymore. Tony is busy at the hospital, Donna involved with raising money for charities, and the children are all professionals. Nick is a trauma surgeon ("a surgeon *and* a sculptor," his father proudly says); Eliza is a dress and fabric designer, and

Christina is an author whose best-selling novel, *Drowning Ruth,* is nostalgically set on the farm and by the lake. Yet the entire family contributes energy and artistry to the place. The colorful flowers and paint, the artifacts and artwork, are not done for anyone's pleasure but their own. Their hearts are in the farm; it has been preserved by them and renewed with a contemporary spirit. It reflects their creativity, their playfulness, and their love of it, inside and out. This is what gives it soul. It is a place of Wisconsin, of its past and its present, celebrated and enjoyed by the Meyer family for its history and its varied settings of farmland, oak wood, and lake.

LEFT: Here, under the oaks, architect David Kahler built the Meyers' year-round residence to recall the barns and silos that are so much a part of the Wisconsin landscape.

RIGHT: A woodland of native oak and hickory comprises a part of the homestead. Its edges are planted with indigenous ferns, viburnum, and snakeroot, which complement Nick Meyer's sculpture of an unfurling ostrich fern.

ROBERT JAKOB

Cottage Gardening on Long Island

Like many gardeners who have toiled in the same garden for twenty years or more, Robert Jakob looks at his flowery expanse and talks about paring down, about the beauty and ease of a landscape made up solely of boxwood and trees. But then, he says wistfully, "I wouldn't have these"—waving his hand across the tangle of annuals, bulbs, perennials, herbs, and roses that give his garden its joyful spirit.

Walk through the south-facing French doors of his cottage near Long Island's Acabonack Harbor on an August day, and you are immediately enveloped in undulating, dancing flowers. Snakeroot sways above stands of sky blue *Salvia uliginosa* and dark blue *Salvia guaranitica*, slender-petaled daylilies in deep red and clear yellow mingle with dill and *Verbena bonariensis*, purple fennel smokes behind orange torch lilies and red lobelia, garlic chives weave in and out of white prickly poppies (*Argemone mexicana*), and pale flowers of gaura flutter like butterflies along the edges of the paths. Although the immediate impression is delight at the seemingly unorchestrated profusion of plants, you see quickly that an underlying structure keeps the garden from any sense of chaos. Bluestone paths crisscross through the verdancy, creating perspectives, their geometry accentuated by a repetitive use of certain good-foliaged plants. Clumps of gray-green sage, the bold, round-leaf form called *Salvia officinalis* 'Berggarten' occur at intervals along edges of the borders, as do sheaves of iris. Great, round, mounded bushes of dwarf English box, four feet high and deliciously pungent in the summer sun, are paired

A cinderblock cottage was transformed by covering it with shingle and lattice. The raspberry-pink flowers of *Rosa rugosa rubra,* poppies, and blue larkspurs flower in June. Clematis and the climber 'Sombreuil' clothe the house wall.

TOP: The living room French doors open into the garden where a bluestone path leads past boxwood and a profusion of flowers.

BOTTOM: Outside the living room, pots of lemons and bay are staged in summer.

OPPOSITE: In the sandy acid soil of the Dry Garden, iris, sage, thyme, and the brilliant orange butterfly weed native to Eastern meadows, *Asclepias tuberosa,* thrive.

along the paths, giving the garden weight and structure. Stands of old red cedars, the native *Juniperus virginiana,* provide a suitably somber backdrop.

Cedars were littering the place when Robert and his partner, David White, bought the three-and-a-half-acre property in 1980. Robert, who was working as a graphic designer in New York City at the time, and David, who is the curator for Robert Rauschenberg, were looking for a weekend cottage. The small cinderblock one-room house, painted a glossy white, choked by brambles and half-dead cedars, had potential to their imaginative eyes. The house wasn't winterized, so Robert and David added insulation, then covered the concrete on the outside of the one-story building with lath strips and shingle. The facade of the house very quickly faded to a weathered gray, and with its tracery of ramblers and clematis, looked settled enough to be historic. Shingled houses, after all, have been the vernacular here on the East End of Long Island since colonial days.

Very quickly, Robert and David realized they needed more space indoors. In 1985 they decided to build an addition for two bedrooms. They thought at length about what they could add on to something so unassuming. They settled on a tower. "It was the look of the houses out here," Robert says, referring to the old shingled windmills seen throughout

ON FARMLAND

LEFT: Robert and David fashioned a deer fence out of one-inch by two-inch spruce laths and let it weather.

RIGHT: A tower, inspired in part by local windmills, was added to the small house to provide more bedroom space.

the Hamptons. Another inspiration, besides the windmills, was the hot-dog stand (Joe's Dog Stand) in the shape of a tower on the public beach in nearby Amagansett. And Robert remembered a beautiful hunting lodge he'd seen in the Dolomites in Italy with two towers that were very squat and had windows all around. He liked their heaviness and thickness. The resulting two-story shingled tower Robert designed to attach to their cottage is not at all ethereal or princely looking, but substantial and appealingly squat, complementing the low structure it adjoins. "We didn't want to destroy what was here," he says. Windows extend around all four sides of the tower, so that the upstairs bedroom is flooded with light and has views of the garden and a sliver of harbor in the distance. "There's something enticing about going *up* into a room," Robert says.

By the time the addition was built, Robert had given up his graphic-design business and settled in the house full time to concentrate on his artwork and the garden. He and David had already spent long hours and weekends hacking away at the briars and cutting down the dead cedars. Healthy cedars were left, and new cedars were planted along the south

boundary to screen the neighbor's house and serve as a backdrop for the garden. The long, narrow property was originally farmland, used for growing melons and obviously for grazing, as they found barbed wire as they cleared. "Traditionally they had cattle here in winter," Robert said. "Then in summer they drove them up to Montauk." (Paintings of the area by William Merritt Chase, who had an art school in Southampton in the late nineteenth century, depict cows and sheep.) The far end of the property is now meadow graced with shad trees (*Amelanchier canadensis*) and blueberries. The meadow borders a wide salt marsh; beyond it is Acabonack Harbor. "David wanted so much to have a little water view," says Robert. "But I did not so much. I wanted a square where I could plant things that were edible or a pleasure to look out on."

Robert grew up in Germany knowing gardens. "The first year here, I just remembered my father's garden and my aunt's. My uncle was a landscape architect. He had a passion for plants. You would take a walk with him and he would say look at that tiny thing on the ground. His eyes were always on the ground observing things." When Robert started his

LEFT: A swath of lawn through high grass leads from the house to the end of the garden and an American beech tree. A cross axis leading into the flower borders is marked by box bushes.

RIGHT: Robert created an allée with hornbeam hedges. "It's not grand, but it is based on grand ideas," Robert says of the garden's axial design.

garden here on Long Island, he took his cue from what he observed around him. Native cedars were an obvious beginning, and the new ones he and David planted as the frame of the garden repeated others already on the property, giving the whole a thread of continuity. Shrubs that they found naturalized near the marsh were repeated in other areas of the garden—bayberries, blueberries, and spice bush (*Lindera benzoin*). "You can't fail if you continue the native planting," Robert says. "Then slowly take on exotic plants. This would be very good advice for anyone starting a garden."

Down bluestone paths, following a central axis from the living room French doors, Robert added one small square garden after another, filling each with flowers and herbs. In one, vegetables are featured in a pattern of beds; another area—his sunniest—is the dry garden, planted with brilliant orange butterfly weed (*Asclepias tuberosa*), irises, sage, creeping thymes, small-flowered poppies, silver-leaved cardoons, and caryopteris, all of which thrive in the sandy soil. Robert is a master at mixed plantings, artfully combining shrubs, herbs, and flowers, many of them uncommon cultivars he seeks out, such as African foxgloves, purple-leaved winter honeysuckle, wild roses, and species peonies. Magnolias (*M. denudata*,

OPPOSITE: Scarlet *Rosa moyesii* blooms profusely behind bearded iris and poppies.

LEFT: The bold-leaved culinary sage, *Salvia officinalis* 'Berggarten' is a constant along the front borders of Robert's garden.

RIGHT: Tall slender-petaled daylilies flower with snakeroot beneath an ornamental cherry tree.

Butter yellow *Phlomis russeliana* consorts with tansy and blue cranesbills.

M. cylindrica, and the cultivar 'Elizabeth') add shade and grace. Tall hornbeam hedges form an allée between the front flowery garden outside the doors of the house and the sunny back garden.

The heart of the garden, what grounds it and gives it its richness and substance, is the boxwood. Robert uses fat, round bushes of box repeatedly, in the beds or in pots, marking the entrance to paths and drawing your eye along them, giving weight to the flower beds, highlighting the ephemeral blooms with their shadowy darkness. It is this contrast of solid, dense, dark globes with loose, light-hearted, brightly colored flowers that is so satisfying.

The intensely planted flower garden radiates out from the south side of Robert and David's cottage. To the east, another set of French doors in the living room are flung open in summer to a long, narrow stretch of lawn and beyond it, the meadow and marsh. The lawn is simply bordered on both sides by high grass and clumps of bayberry. To the left, a small, shingled building is nestled in among tall cedars. This is Robert's studio, originally a cabin at a boys' camp, which he and David salvaged and brought home. They raised the ceiling, added two tiers of small-paned windows, shingled it, and covered it with the rambling Tea-Noisette 'Alister Stella Gray'—its clusters of pale yellow flowers lovely in summer against the silvery wood. The charming China rose 'Mutabilis', barely hardy here in Zone 7, survives on the sheltered south side of the studio, its canes of single flowers, colored pale yellow to pink to crimson, "trying to come in the windows."

The lawn leads down past the studio, past a Persian walnut, which shades a small café table and two chairs, to an American beech tree and a teak bench on the edge of the meadow. Behind the bench, a seven-foot-high open lattice fence divides the lawn from the meadow. David and Robert built the fence out of spruce, using two-by-twos, to enclose the garden and keep out deer. Beyond the fence, paths are cut through the high meadow grasses past clumps of bayberries and blueberries and colonies of graceful shad. The shad, Robert said, are all the same age. They came up naturally after the land was no longer used for grazing. Native tupelo trees (*Nyssa sylvatica*) picturesquely border the edge of the marsh. David keeps the meadow cleared of catbriar—the local weed—and tends the trees and shrubs here. "He is the guardian of the wetlands," Robert says. Both men are upset that phragmites is taking over the salt marsh. Its tall fronds will eventually hide David's small wedge of harbor view.

Everywhere in the garden are places to sit. Benches, a hammock, chairs beneath a tree, or in the shade of a grapevine arbor offer places to pause, have tea or a meal. In the meadow by the marsh, a log seat faces a vista cut in the grass to some distant trees. "The view announced itself,"

The rambler rose 'Alister Stella Gray' and autumn clematis climb over the studio Robert and David salvaged from a boys' camp nearby. Bayberry bushes and an old native cedar give it an air of permanence.

The verticals of native Eastern Cedars, rounded bushes of bayberry, and boxwood define the garden in winter as well as summer.

said Robert, whose eye saw beauty in the trees' outlines, and so he cleared and edited accordingly. Looking and editing are the keys to success in a garden such as Robert and David's, to keep it from becoming overgrown and jumbled. There's a fine line between not wanting a garden to look too orderly and having it get out of control. The best gardens, like Robert's, are edited with an artist's eye, deleting and simplifying here, letting Nature have its way there, allowing and delighting in the unexpected when it seems right—those serendipitous combinations of flowers, for instance, that occur from unintentional seeding and interweaving. The trick is to keep a clarity of view. "You can take something that looks quite neglected and make it sparkling by taking things out," Robert said—a truth that comes only with experience.

The East End of Long Island has a long, rich history of resident artists, from Childe Hassam and William Merritt Chase to Jackson Pollack. It has an even longer history of cottage gardens, with its sea air, mild climate, and often humus-rich soil. The earliest settlers began that history with their patterned plots of boxwood and flowering herbs. Larger, more ambitiously formal gardens proliferated here during the Golden Age at the turn of the twentieth century, but dooryard gardens flourished as well and were recorded by American Impressionist artists of the time who flocked to the area. Drive down village streets here today, and you will

catch glimpses of flowery yards. Many contemporary artists, like Robert, live in these neighborhoods and have turned their talents to the earth. Some of the resulting gardens are defined by sculpture, but others, like Robert's, are memorable updated versions of the traditional cottage garden. Robert's place will perhaps be simplified in the years to come, but it will continue to charm visitors with its boxwood and native red cedars, blueberries, roses, and magnolias, interwoven with an inevitable medley of flowers that will persist without coddling—the poppies, gaura, foxgloves, violas, verbena, lobelias, fennel, and snakeroot that, unaided, will seed themselves about the beds.

The structural plants, or "bones" of Robert's garden—its deciduous trees, evergreen cedars, boxwood, and twiggy shrubs and hedges—are enhanced by a covering of snow.

Eastern Woodland

If you live and garden in woodland, it is best to let go of any dream of sun-filled beds of roses, and revel instead in the possibilities of a shade garden. This can be difficult, I know, given an almost universal desire for sunshine and flowers. But if you high-prune your trees, and thin out ones where they are crowded, you can have flowers—all those enchanting spring ephemerals, bulbs, and perennials that flourish in rich humus and dappled shade. Visit the woodland garden at Winterthur, in Delaware, with its hillsides of winter aconites, windflowers, and colchicums; or Garden in the Woods, in Massachusetts, where drifts of spring phlox and foam flower paint the forest floor blue and white in May; or the Asticou Azalea Garden in Maine, carpeted with bunchberries and wild ginger, and the most stubborn worshipper of sun-drenched borders will be convinced that there are rich pleasures in gardening beneath trees.

Our Eastern woodland is startlingly beautiful even without the aid of flowers. Beech, maple, oak, dogwood, hemlock, and pine clothe its gentle slopes. The ground is littered with lichen-crusted granite boulders; clear, rock-strewn streams cut through its valleys. Moss blankets the ground and ferns colonize in the dampness.

The gardeners in the following pages, who live in such woodland, have come to appreciate the beauty of *green*. Flowers are incidental in their gardens; textures and patterns of green are what interest them. Their woodland settings provide the serenity they seek. The predominance of foliage in their gardens results in a simplicity they find fitting.

A stream was brought alive by a series of
small stone dams in a Delaware woodland garden.

ROXANA ROBINSON

Maine Retreat

Mount Desert Island in northern
Maine differs from most other large islands along
the New England seacoast, by being mountainous,
granite-strewn, and densely wooded with spruce and pine. Nantucket,
Fisher's Island, Long Island, and North Haven (I have never been to
Martha's Vineyard), with their stretches of fields and, at most, a gently
rolling terrain, give the impression of openness and sunlight. Mount
Desert, in contrast, is shadowy and mysterious, painted in dark, rich
greens. Its scenery is unusually dramatic for the East Coast—majestic
rather than pastoral, with craggy bluffs plunging into a cold blue sea and
lichen-mottled ledge rock littering the forest hillsides, which are richly
clothed with moss, bunchberry, and fern.

The appeal of the island's wild land and water, as well as its relaxed
way of life, brought novelist Roxana Robinson and her husband, Tony, to
the island year after year, and convinced them finally to buy a few acres of
their own. The five-acre parcel, thickly wooded with white pine, red and
white spruce, red maple, and oak, sloped down to a secluded tidal cove
where Roxana, a dedicated observer of wildlife, knew birds and creatures
must congregate. For two years the Robinsons kept the land without
building; they had a full, busy life in New York, and Roxana was hesitant
to take on the responsibility of another home. Finally, they "plunged for-
ward" with dreams of a home that would serve as a refuge, and a garden
that would flourish in the mountain-sea air.

It was hard at first to imagine a house and
garden on the land, Roxana says. "The under-
story of a coniferous forest is just dead

An interior garden, planted by
landscape architect Patrick
Chassé, features a medley of
textures and patterns of green.

branches. Scrambling around with my eyes shut, it was just like walking through a closet with the lights off." Roxana and Tony wisely called upon two experts for help: the Boston architect Jim Righter (who happened to be Tony's brother-in-law) and Mount Desert's well-known landscape architect, Patrick Chassé. Both men are known for a sensitivity to their surroundings; their designs, the Robinsons knew, would be in the context of this northern Maine island, as well as suit the specific site. But first the technical challenges had to be dealt with. Patrick recalls the difficulty he and Jim Righter had siting the house. "It was such a thicket of unkempt woods (two- and three-inch-diameter evergreens growing three feet apart), you couldn't see for more than twenty feet. You could hear the road, and you knew the shore was opposite the road, and from that you had to try to figure how the house would fit with imaginary views." Two brooks ran parallel to the shore across the property, which made the siting even more complicated. Their solution, finally, was to build the house over one of the brooks, which now disappears under the

foundation in a big drain and emerges on the other side like a natural spring.

Jim Righter is known not only as an architect who cares about the appropriateness of what he builds, but as a designer with an imaginative sense of fun. He knew the Robinsons desired a house big enough for them, their children, and grandchildren, but with the air of a camp. And Roxana wanted a tower where she could write. She also wanted the place to look as if it might have been there since the turn of the twentieth century. To gather ideas, Jim suggested they spend a weekend driving around Mount Desert Island so Roxana could point out her favorite buildings. They looked at the long, low, slanting roofline, the boldly jutting rafters, and the spacious porch of the old Northeast Harbor Tennis Club. Jim interpreted these features in the Robinsons' low-slung house, the swoop of its roof almost Oriental in feeling, its porch generous and comfortable. They noted the proportions of the great room at the Golf Club, which suggested the dimensions of their own large living room. Best of all, Roxana

showed Jim St. Jude's Church in Seal Harbor, built by William Ralph Emerson in the 1870s. In its details, Jim found the quintessential spirit of what he wanted to achieve in the Robinsons' house. The small, gray-shingled structure has a playful rusticity with its curiously waving, sometimes conical roof lines. The "candle-snuffer hood," or ogee roof, over the entrance door of the church, which embraces the church bell and shelters the visitor, is whimsically echoed above the front door Jim designed for the Robinsons. A series of small windows in the church's arcade inspired similar windows in an arcade overlooking Roxana's garden. The glossy, black-green paint of the church's windows, rafters, and doors, a color often used on the island's structures, is repeated in the dark wood details of the new shingled house. And, just as you enter the church door to find you are not yet in the church proper, but only in an entryway, so Jim devised the Robinsons' entrance door as a playful pretense. You enter the door under the candle snuffer roof to discover you aren't yet in the house at all, but in a garden.

At first, Roxana—who is a gardener as well as a lover of nature—thought of having a colorful flower garden at her new home. Lavish flower borders, set in clearings in the woods, are indeed a common, if sometimes startling, feature on Mount Desert Island. The precedent was established in the 1920s by Abby Aldrich Rockefeller when she and her husband, John D. Rockefeller Jr., asked landscape gardener Beatrix Farrand to design a vast garden of perennials and annuals at their wooded summer place, The Eyrie, high above Seal Harbor. But the more Roxana thought about her new home, about its being so far away in the north, the more she imagined it in her mind's eye as "distant, northern, cool, peaceful," the less she wanted roses, lilies, phloxes, or delphiniums. "I decided

I wanted a garden that looked very different than the classic lush border. No reds, no rose colors, no deep blues. In fact I didn't want any color at all." What she wanted was something that spoke of silence, refuge. "I realized finally I didn't want any flowers at all. Foliage was more nurturing, deeper, more mysterious. This was a huge epiphany for me."

Roxana knew what she wanted but not how to achieve it. Bare dirt around a freshly built house is a daunting prospect, especially if you live far away most of the year. Consequently, she felt fortunate to have Patrick to do the design of the garden. "He's a genius with foliage. It's his turf, he knows the plants, he understands the land, and how I feel about the environment." Indeed, northern Maine is Pat's cherished home ground. Here as elsewhere, he combines a botanist's knowledge of woodland flora with an artist's eye for pattern and texture.

The house is T-shaped; in its angle, enclosed by a high fence of shingle and lattice, Roxana was to have her patterned garden of foliage. It would be a mixture of native and non-native plants. Beyond the garden walls, however, everything was to be native. "I wanted a place," Roxana says,

OPPOSITE, TOP: Ferns and lungwort are used as an underplanting in the interior garden.

OPPOSITE, BOTTOM: Snakeroot and plume poppies provide vertical interest above *Hosta sieboldiana*.

ABOVE: The entrance to the Robinsons' house with its "candle-snuffer hood" was inspired by a similar entrance door at St. Jude's Church in Seal Harbor. It leads to the interior porch and garden.

Roxana and Lacy, her standard poodle, sit on a porch bench in view of the tidal cove through the woods. The ground around the freshly built house was "skin grafted" with native hay-scented ferns, low-bush blueberry, sweet fern, and bayberry.

"that didn't hold off the surrounding landscape, that wasn't severed from the setting. I wanted to feel that we were connected to the rest of the landscape." A thirty-foot-wide band around the house and its walled garden was replanted with native shrubs and groundcovers, "like skin grafting a burn," Patrick says. Colonies of bayberry, sweet fern, drifts of hay-scented fern, and low-bush blueberry now soften the house and entrance drive. Whenever possible, the plants are fruiting and berrying, Roxana notes, "so they play an active part in the landscape." As a rule in welcoming wildlife, no poisonous substances are ever to be used. "As for the deer," that bane of so many gardeners, "the wall keeps them out of the garden. Beyond that, they are welcome to sample anything they like. We have a working relationship."

Between the house and the tidal cove, the big challenge for Pat was creating more light and opening vistas by carefully thinning the woods. "It was such a rat's nest," Pat remembers, but clear cutting near the water was not allowed. Pat worked patiently with the planning board of the

The entrance porch encloses one side of the lavishly planted interior garden.

town: "We marked off fifty-by-fifty-foot blocks and thinned each one by a different formula for their consideration." In the end, the board agreed to the most ambitious thinning. That, Pat believes, was a blessing. A variety of native groundcovers were planted after the thinning to ensure the long-term health of the woodland. Existing shrubs—mostly bayberries—were preserved along the shore. That natural fringe makes creatures feel safe; here fox and coyotes, as well as birds, linger by the water's edge.

On the side of the house away from the shore, Pat carved out a space for a small meadow of local wildflowers and grasses. Roxana wanted more light between the house and the deep woods, but she had no desire for a lawn. There were to be no mowers and blowers "racketing about the property, no horrible, deadly weed wackers" disrupting that feeling of silence she cherished. Instead, the wildflowers bring insects and birds, the sort of activity Roxana advocates on her land.

Roxana enjoys a more studied garden nestled against the house within the shingled and latticed walls. Here, in an area forty-five by thirty-five

Fragrant clethra, snakeroot, Solomon's seal, and plume poppies offer quiet white flowers.

feet, shaded by tall white pines, Pat designed a dramatically patterned tapestry of foliage in hues of gray and green. Gradually, a few pale flowers have crept in, but the effect remains one of coolness, serenity, shadow, and light. Billowing elders, tall feathering rowans, the statuesque plume poppy, heracleum, as well as clethra and shrub dogwood, give the garden a strong structure. On a lower plane, astilbes mingle with ferns (cinnamon, royal, hay-scented, and ostrich), Japanese anemones, peppermint geraniums, lamiums, native gingers, tiarellas, and bunchberry. Goat's beard, snakeroot, Solomon's seal, thalictrums, and filipendulas give height and a contrasting delicacy. Hostas (*H. sieboldiana* and 'Blue Mammoth') and petasites add powerful strokes of light and shade with their huge heart-shaped leaves. A single path of shredded bark wends gently through the garden from the house to a gate in the high fence. A millstone, inspired by one at Garland Farm, Beatrix Farrand's final garden on Mount Desert Island, is set in the center of the path where it widens to a circle.

The house Jim designed embraces this small, lushly planted woodland courtyard in such a way that "you're walking around the garden whether

A large, many-paned window in the Robinsons' living room looks out onto the intimate garden. A gate at the end opens out to the native woodland.

you're inside or outside," he says. Jim's pretend front door—the entrance—opens to a loggia that runs along the side of the house and reveals the leafy garden. At the far end of this loggia is the true front door, which leads to a hallway, or arcade, lit by a series of windows that look out to the garden. At the end of this is what the Robinsons call their "book room," the place where they relax and entertain. It is high-ceilinged and rustic, with a huge stone fireplace. Clerestory windows and a large picture window bring the green garden indoors.

Roxana wonders if her appreciation of this garden has something to do with age. Of course it does. "When I started gardening," she says— and she is speaking for the majority of gardeners, "all I wanted was color. I wasn't interested in shrubs or trees or foliage." Now, many years later, she is enthralled with the idea that leaves are a garden. "When you limit the color palate so drastically, you become aware of subtleties and nuances, textures and patterns. There is something nourishing, sustaining about looking at an all-foliage garden." This garden within the walls, despite its inclusion of Asian plants among the natives, captures the essence of Mount Desert—cool, shadowy, dramatic, and richly, predominately green.

With the creative sensibilities of Jim Righter and Patrick Chassé, Roxana has achieved her goal. Her new home fits seamlessly into its landscape, its atmosphere in tune with the northern woods. It is, as she hoped, a distant place of peacefulness.

Delaware Moss Garden

Rod Ward calls his well-loved acreage in Centerville, Delaware a "one-note garden." What he means by this modest disclaimer is that his garden is not complex, nor about flowers—no cottagelike borders, no rose garden, no parterres filled with annuals, no blazing color; it is, rather, only, and all about green. Set in a valley of climax forest beneath magnificent beeches, oaks, and tulip poplars, it is a landscape of remarkable simplicity and serenity, a vast carpet of mosses and ferns cut through by a meandering stream.

Rod and his wife, Susan, live in the bucolic countryside that straddles northern Delaware and Pennsylvania, a setting made famous by Henry Francis du Pont in his naturalistic garden at Winterthur, three miles away. It is rolling, fertile land, part open fields where great old oaks spread their limbs horizontally, part rich woodland with steep banks and running streams, shaded by our most beautiful Eastern hardwood deciduous trees.

In 1965, Rod and Susan returned from a three-year sojourn in Japan to settle with their young children on land that had been in Rod's family for two generations. His grandmother had died while they were away, and her one-hundred-acre property was being bought up by relatives. By the time Rod and Susan came home, only four acres were left unsold—acres that nobody else in the family wanted. On a family map, Susan recalls, the parcel was called "The Wasteland." Rod knew the spot from his childhood days; he and his brother had "messed around back there in the stream." As a building site, it was a challenge. "The land was on a huge slope, the trees all wrapped in vines. Frankly, we

A smooth swath of lawn leads down from the modernist house to the wooded valley of ferns and moss.

The Wards' house of shingle and glass was designed in the 1960s by architect A. Holmes Stockly and sited to take full advantage of the magnificent woodland panorama. A Japanese snowbell tree (*Styrax japonica*) shades the terrace.

bought it because it was there. We didn't have a lot of money, and we were able to afford it." Moreover, looking beyond the impenetrable thicket of underbrush and wet ground, Rod and Susan saw on their site the intangible beauty of the forest with its towering, ancient trees.

Having come home deeply impressed by Japanese culture and art, they wanted a house influenced by that aesthetic, but suited to its very American surroundings. They asked architect A. Holmes Stockly, who had worked with Philip Johnson, to design a house big enough for their family that would complement their Oriental furnishings and fit comfortably in the landscape. Stockly built a modern, flat-roofed, boxlike dwelling of shingle and ample glass, set into the steep bank above the valley, where it would capture poetic views of sun filtering through woodland. "He had a great eye for beauty," Susan says. Today, the house blends so subtly with its setting, it seems almost like an elegant tree house, jutting out among the towering oaks and beeches.

Holmes Stockly called on his friend, landscape architect Conrad Hammerman, to help with the essential terracing around the house. Retaining walls and steps of native stone were designed to descend from the drive to the house entrance, and huge granite slabs were placed just outside the glass doors of the living room. After a few years, moss developed between the stone slabs, delighting Susan and Rod. Eventually the Wards called on another landscape architect, Richard Vogel, who taught at the University of Pennsylvania, to deal with the steep grade of their site. Vogel

extended the stone terrace outside the living room doors to include a small pool, and planted a graceful Japanese snowbell tree (*Styrax japonica*) to shade its seating area. Beyond the terrace, he cleared an area of trees, then built a long, curving stone retaining wall, which cut into the upper part of the bank and delineated—with the help of forty truckloads of fill—a level area for lawn. Standing at the house, looking out from the terrace, that sweep of lawn affords an open, sunlit space that draws the eye to the woods in the distance and gives a sense of its cathedral-like scale. Above the low arc of wall and lawn, the bank was planted simply and strikingly with masses of cranberry cotoneaster. Below the platform of turf, the land fell down sharply to the valley floor into a tangle of untouched, untamed forest. With their house settled comfortably in its surroundings, the Wards were ready to tackle the woods.

"We were faced with the valley in truly awful shape," Rod recalls. "You couldn't walk through at first," because of fallen trees and brush and vines. "We had no master plan; we cleared one area at a time." The immediate goal was to open vistas while preserving the native understory of the woods. "The fundamental idea was to gain some dimension, some distance." As they cleared, the Wards marked out paths, which they made with the help of Wally Petrol who had been head gardener at Winterthur when H. F. du Pont was alive. Varying in width between two and four feet, they were edged simply with steel and dressed with chipped bark. "It was my view that no path should be straight," Rod says. Today, they curve gently and enticingly along both sides of a stream that runs and spills over

Planting boxes outside the dining room windows, called window gardens, were originally planted with astilbes, ginger, hellebores, liriope, acorus, and *Iris cristata* but reduced finally to the simplicity of moss and rocks.

TOP: Steps lead down through a carpet of ferns.

BOTTOM: The various native mosses Rod plants come from within a mile's radius. He brings home a small turf of moss, weeds it, wets it into a slurry, then cuts it like cookies and plants it. With regular watering the moss spreads naturally.

a series of dams through the bottom of the valley. "It was a nasty little stream, more a ditch," Rod remembers. "We wondered what would happen if we dammed it up." Rod and Wally put in the first dam one summer while Susan was away. "When I came home, I was transfixed at how pretty it was," she says. Delighted with its success, they made dams in eleven places along the winding stream, varying in height from eighteen inches to two feet, using stone, but no cement. The small dams cause the water to come alive, falling with gentle noise along its course. "It never dries up," Rod says, "There's always a trickle." Wooden bridges were built to cross the stream, and simple wooden steps made out of old railroad ties ("not the new pressure-treated kind") were set into the banks where needed.

Having cleared and established trails, Rod set about planting the ground. Looking around him, recognizing the power of the mature woodland and the serenity it afforded, Rod decided to concentrate on the native ferns and mosses that were evidently at home here. He chose ferns particularly because "they're easy to grow in this dark, damp valley. And I like their textures." What he did, which was masterly, was to plant each sort of fern in great breathtaking sweeps. Perhaps he was influenced by his neighbor, garden designer Bill Frederick, who advocates planting in bold strokes and advised Rod periodically on the garden. (Bill's vast, swooping carpets of brilliantly colored shrubs and groundcovers in his own garden recall in scale and color the style of Burle Marx.) Longwood Gardens nearby was another inspiration with its densely planted carpets of ferns. Pamela Copeland's marvelous shade garden of native Piedmont flora, Mt. Cuba, and Winterthur, were other neighboring models.

Rod massed ten different native ferns in areas along the stream and down the wooded slopes: lady fern ("the local weed fern"), all the Osmunda family—royal, cinnamon, and interrupted, the delicate beech fern, Christmas fern ("Christmas ferns love a slope," Rod says), maiden-hair, New York fern, ostrich, and hay-scented. ("Tan-tan-ta-ra," Susan laughingly describes the sight of hay-scented ferns coming down an incline, for "they look like they're marching on us.") Some of the ferns that Rod spread along his walks come from his own wooded property, which has grown to twenty acres over the years. Ten acres are deer-fenced with eight-foot-high black plastic netting to protect the natural under-story, but only three are intensely gardened. Rod buys other ferns from a wholesale nursery in North Carolina. "I buy them by the hundreds. They come bare-root, for eighty-five cents. You can't kill them," he says.

As a contrast to the patterned sweeps of ferns, reaching down to the stream and along walkways, Rod planted and encouraged velvet carpets of moss. More than a dozen different kinds of moss have settled in over the years. "All the mosses are native," Rod says, "and came from within a mile of here. I go out with a bag, and when I see the moss, I take a turf of it [a small piece], scoop it up, repair the damage, put it in trays, make it wet, smoosh it, then cut it like cookies and plant it." With time, the patches fill in to make a whole. A lot of moss also occurs naturally. Generous paths of this rich plush green have gradually replaced grass where the ground is shaded near the house. Moss now spreads its blanket beneath towering tulips and oaks above the stream. It laps over the roots of trees and clothes fallen trunks along the woodland walks. "It's nicer, softer than a lawn," Rod states. "Lawns are always getting things wrong with them."

TOP AND BOTTOM: Ten different native ferns, including New York, ostrich, cinnamon, inter-rupted, beech, and maiden-hair, are planted in great sweeps under the beeches and oaks.

Christmas ferns blanket the sloping ground, and the stream is bordered by masses of lady ferns, considered to be the local weed.

(This, of course, is the raison d'être of chemical lawn companies.) The Wards have the perfect habitat for mossy ground, namely acid woodland soil that is shaded and damp. But Rod helps it to flourish with regular irrigation. "You can't over-water moss; it needs to stay damp." In nature, Rod reminds me, moss looks miserable in August and September after a typically dry summer. "We irrigate it at night, for twenty minutes, from a deep well on our property. We had the good luck to find this water." With this regime, which he follows from April through November, Rod keeps his garden looking green and lush through the growing season. "It even looks kind of nice in the winter," he adds modestly.

Other species of native woodland flora add their textures to this garden of green. Skunk cabbage fills swales where the ground is wet; dog-tooth violets crop up through the moss, partridge berry creeps around the roots of beeches, may apples appear in colonies in spring. Native dog-woods (*Cornus florida*) abound here, our most treasured Eastern under-story tree. Rod occasionally adds more young specimens of dogwoods

along the walks. Near the house, however, not all the plantings are native. A dwarf Japanese maple weeps picturesquely by the terrace outside the living room doors. The snowbell tree, now full-grown and fountaining over a cluster of teak chairs and table, anchors its far end. On one particularly troublesome bank that tumbles precipitously down from the house, Rod replaced part of a massed planting of Christmas ferns with pachysandra to hold the soil. "I don't care," he says defensively, knowing how we plant snobs react to this ubiquitous Asian groundcover, "I like pachysandra. It stops water dead in its track and allows it to soak into the ground." The Wards are perfectly happy to have a few appropriate Asian plants near the house, but they are careful to plant only natives in the woodland valley.

What Rod and Susan have achieved with their thoughtful clearing and planting of quiet expanses of ferns and moss is an aura of peacefulness, a sense of calm. They have merely enhanced their ravishingly beautiful native Delaware woodland. While honoring their love of a Japanese aesthetic, they built a very American house and nurtured an American

Stone dams were built in eleven places along the steam, which was originally little more than a wet ditch.

EASTERN WOODLAND

landscape. This garden captures the feeling of a Japanese garden in its tranquility and simplicity, while staying true to its place and time. "Do not follow in the footsteps of men of old," advises the seventeenth-century Japanese poet Bashō. "Seek what they sought."

With grown children and retirement from a busy law practice approaching, Susan and Rod seem to revel in the quiet work of gardening. Weeding moss is a solitary, contemplative occupation they both enjoy. Pruning, picking up sticks, removing the leaves in fall ("a tremendous job"), putting down mulch in spring—"all the stuff I can't stand to do," Rod says, are left to their once-a-week gardener, Joe. "To be blunt," Rod says, "there's an enormous amount of maintenance in this carefree garden. I hope it doesn't show."

The specter of high maintenance doesn't stop true gardeners like Rod and Susan. They not only plant and weed; they plot new paths, and designate new stretches of woods to tend. Their newest project is a pond in a very low wet spot beyond the deer fencing. They intend to plant native berrying shrubs there for the birds—viburnums, aronias, shrub dogwoods, and winterberries; and they talk of extending the deer netting. What their "one-note" garden shows in its air of serenity, its textured carpets of green, its shadows and light, is Rod and Susan's nurturing presence, their passionate, intimate involvement in the land.

OPPOSITE AND ABOVE: By clearing vines and brush, selectively cutting and high-pruning the great beeches and oaks, sunlight and a sense of space were introduced to the wooded property, accentuating its cathedral-like quality. Inspired by a Japanese aesthetic applied to their own beautiful native woodland, the Wards have created a serene and elegantly understated American garden.

In the Southern Tradition

History and tradition are so embedded in the landscape and architecture of the South that they are often as important an influence on its gardens as the climate and the soil. The early settlers brought the English and Dutch aesthetics—their love of formalism, their use of boxwood, their patterned gardens of roses and herbs—to the southern colonies in the seventeenth century. The fertility of the land and the abundance of slave labor led to great agrarian wealth in the eighteenth century; its cultured, worldly gentry created elegant and sophisticated town houses, manors, and plantations exemplified by Jefferson's Monticello in Virginia and the splendid Middleton Place in Charleston. The devastation during the Civil War left its own indelible traces—towns burned, forests cut, great houses destroyed or let to fade, gardens abandoned and gone wild. All these threads are part of the fabric of the South today.

So is the climate. The summers are hot and humid. Drought is often a worry, as are deluges of rain. Nevertheless, a wealth of plants flourishes. North Carolinian Elizabeth Lawrence, one of America's best loved garden authors of the twentieth century, writes,

"In the South the progress of the seasons does not follow the accepted pattern of spring, summer, fall, and winter. The garden year has no beginning and no end. To follow the tradition of bloom in three seasons only is to miss the full meaning of gardening in a part of the world where at all times of the year there are days when it is good to be out of doors, when there is work to be done in the garden, and when there is some plant in perfection of flower or fruit."

The two gardeners profiled in the following pages would agree. Each of them has absorbed Southern history, its sense and its style, and breathed new life into it. One gardener, in Virginia, takes that history and tradition and reinterprets it, making it her own. The other, in Charleston, is devoted to rescuing the old plants of the South and restoring them to prominence.

The climbing Tea-Noisette rose 'Rêve d'Or' tumbles down from a serpentine brick wall at Boone Hall outside of Charleston, South Carolina.

MARY McCONNELL

Virginia Style

I<small>T IS EASY TO MISS THE ENTRANCE TO</small> Mary and Jamie McConnell's place, Summer Duck Wood, in Orange County, Virginia. A few numbers written on a small wood stake along the main road mark the turn-off. A drive of rutted gravel wends through thick woods for three-quarters of a mile, then suddenly opens to a sunlit field of high grass. A series of ponds with islands on them masked with wild shrubbery are to one side; on the other are farm buildings and the kennels where the McConnells' twenty-five English setters and seven horses are housed. From the field a circle of young oaks leads into a graveled parking area, and finally to the stone house, its cream-colored, bowed front welcoming, a tangle of flowers within its embrace. Nothing, however, is more welcoming than Mary, fresh from the garden dressed in pants, boots, and a straw hat, clippers in hand, surrounded by her loyal court of dogs, her face flushed and sparkling with joie de vivre. Her enthusiasm is infectious as are her ideas and the love she feels for this place where she lives.

Mary and her husband, Jamie, are devoted to the well-being of their land and their animals—not just the dogs and horses, but the wild creatures, the birds and the fauna that live in their woods and fields. Summer Duck Wood is a fifteen-hundred-acre piece of rolling, rich Virginia woods and meadows. It is a hunting park and wildlife preserve as well as their home. Over half of the property is wooded—mostly oak (seven different species) with some spruce, and, in low areas, green ash and sycamore. "It has always been woods," Jamie says. "It was never tilled." But the Union Army camped here after Gettysburg—

White-flowering camassia and bearded iris bloom with gray-leaved lychnis in the kitchen garden.

three hundred thousand soldiers—and few trees in the woods survived their stay. Today's young native forest is lovingly nurtured by Jamie, who is more interested in overseeing the natural succession of the trees than in harvesting them. The open fields are not hayed or grazed by cattle, but kept wild as cover for birds. "Our pleasure and goal," Jamie says, "is to maintain a natural wildlife habitat." The McConnells hunt deer on their land as part of a Virginia state management program—they cull thirty does a year, thereby balancing the native population—and shoot geese, woodcock, wild turkey, rabbit, and squirrel. Nevertheless, the wild creatures, as well as the native flora, are nurtured. "For all the images of brutality associated with human hunters in recent decades, they are the ones who know the land, know the animals intimately, and care for the animals they hunt," Mary says. "True hunters have a sense of communion with land and animals." In tending the land, Jamie mows fields on a three-to-five-year rotation, and cuts panels of grass to promote the well-being of wild quail and turkey. He and Mary train their champion field-trial setters to hunt quail on the property, shooting blanks when the dogs point. Seventeen wood duck boxes, made by Jamie, appear at intervals at the woodland's edge. Bear, bobcat, turkey, quail, wild ducks, and song birds abound.

"We know this land intimately—the plants and the animals and the shapes that hold them,"

A stone path outside the master bedroom leads to an outdoor shower hidden within a circle of clipped hornbeam, which boasts the same proportions as Jefferson's rotunda at the University of Virginia.

IN THE SOUTHERN TRADITION

Mary tells me. "I know the swales that hold the snow the longest in winter and where to go to get out of the wind. I know where to ford the streams on horseback and where to stop for a picnic in the woods. I know the owl that swoops over the woodland roads and the geese that nest beside the ponds, and how many eggs were hatched in each wood duck box that Jamie built, and placed, and tends each spring."

Indeed, it was the land, not a house, they fell in love with in 1988. Mary and Jamie were living at the time in Charlottesville while Mary finished her doctorate in anthropology. "Our house there was in town and we loved being near the University of Virginia, but I couldn't grow lilies in that garden because it was so shady and the house was bursting at the seams

The McConnells built five ponds with islands and surrounded them with native flowers and shrubs to encourage bird life. Their acid clay soil, Jamie says, is perfect for pond making.

Achillea 'Coronation Gold', alliums, foxtail lilies (*Eremurus* sp.), and golden *Kerria* in the kitchen garden visually separate the house from the Piedmont countryside beyond.

with books." They decided to look for a place in the Piedmont region of Virginia. "We knew we wanted enough land to have a wild place and knew we wanted good water and soil." At first, their search was frustrating. "So many of the houses that we looked at had a grandeur to them that didn't interest us and not enough land to compensate." On the same day they were shown a grand red brick house with white columns and double drawing rooms, they were also shown this vast, wild acreage with no buildings on it. It had small fields with thick hedgerows framed by a young hickory-oak forest, plenty of natural water, and, in one secluded

Bearded iris, lilies, and purple-leaved smoke bush (*Cotinus coggyria*) border a stone path that circles the house. The McConnells sited their new house on a knoll surrounded by great oak trees.

meadow, a knoll surrounded by large oak trees. "Once we stood under the oaks, we knew this was the land we wanted." They bought it and spent the next four years building a house.

Mary and Jamie called on Virginia architect Thomas Craven to design them a house that would suit their active lifestyle and have a sense of Virginia tradition without being a slavish reconstruction from another era. "When we built the house," Mary says, "we said we wanted this to be our Virginia place in the time in which we are living. In a way, that was our narrative." One decision was to build the house of local fieldstone, not brick, which would be more typical and historically accurate, but seemed too formal. "I think it is the stone that changes the feel of the building," Mary says. Their decision was influenced to some extent by their love of the stonework that is the vernacular for buildings in the Brandywine Valley of Pennsylvania and Delaware where they each grew up. And Mary was inspired by a picture she tore out of a magazine and gave to Tommy Craven of a stone house with arched dormers and roses clambering up its walls, in a graveled courtyard in England. Fittingly, it turned out to be the Coach House at Little Haseley, the utterly charming final home of the renowned decorator and diehard Virginian, Nancy Lancaster, who was Craven's friend and neighbor when she lived at her family place, Mirador, in the Blue Ridge foothills west of Charlottesville. Mary and Jamie had no interest in copying the Coach House, but they liked its spirit. Its quality of graceful proportions and rustic strength pervades their own house.

It is reminiscent in style of eighteenth-century Virginia architecture, a simplified Georgian five-part house, hip-roofed, with symmetrical wings on each side. The tall central portion, topped with a cupola, has small-paned dormers cut into the slate roof above the entrance doorway; it connects to low-roofed passageways on each side, like hyphens, that end with two small hip-roofed pavilions. "What was unusual about the five-part construction was that we curved it. It is half an octagon," Mary says, adding that octagons are "a very Jeffersonian thing."

The curve of the south-facing house creates a natural courtyard, which could have been made quite formal with evergreens and parterres. Instead, Mary filled it to brimming with flowers. The first impression is of a lavishness of flowers, of color and scent, a tangle of roses, lilies, lavender, sages, catmint, and pinks. It has the same air of luxurious exuberance as Mary does herself. There is structure within the tangle, however—bushes of boxwood mark the central path ("Boxwood," Mary says, "is at the heart of the Virginia garden"), and five pear trees add height; figs and quince grow against the walls, and tall cypress frame the front door. There is also a pattern of broad stone paths that leads the eye as well as the foot through the flowers. A straight, seven-foot-wide path runs from the parking area to the front door, and two other narrower paths radiate out at angles to side doors within the building's curves. Another walkway serves as a cross axis, drawing your eye to distant perspectives as it follows along the sides of the house to other gardens and terraces. Mary and Jamie asked landscape architect François Goffinet, who once lived in Charlottesville, to design this hardscaping when the house was built. "Living in the South, he knew the country," Mary says, "and he knew how to feel the space."

The flower garden, with no apology, goes right up to the front door.

Mary is unabashed in her love of flowers. Peonies, lilies, old shrub roses, iris, every sort of small poppy, daffodils—all the blooms that have filled our cottage gardens for the last three centuries delight her. New cultivars catch her fancy too, especially ones that are relatives of native plants she finds on her property. Her house is surrounded by gardens in which she plants these flowers in artful combinations, mingling them with shrubs and then letting them have their head. The front courtyard was her first effort and is her favorite flowery space. "This is the heart of our rooms," she says. Three doors and ten long, gracefully arched, mullioned windows look out onto this front garden, so that it is enjoyed all day at every season. The shrub roses and herbs are underplanted with grape hyacinths and pink and white daffodils for early interest. In May the roses are at their height, blousy sorts like 'Constance Spry' and the very fragrant 'Rosarie de l'Hay', single pink 'Ballerina' and 'Clair Matin'. After the roses fade in the heat of early summer (and the Japanese beetles arrive), the lilies take the stage—delicate species lilies and the more elaborate scented hybrids. Annuals carry the color scheme of pinks, blues, and white here into September, and then the roses start to rebloom. Salvias bloom until winter, and the borders of herbs—such as lavender and lamb's ears—provide good foliage almost year round. "I don't mind when plants go through their stages," Mary says of the moments when some flowers are resting or not looking their best. A little disorder, after all, is part of living.

From her bedroom, Mary has two very different garden views. On the east side, she looks out onto the sunlit flowers in the front courtyard; on the west, she views a shaded garden of white hydrangeas, hellebores, variegated Solomon's seal, ferns, and hostas planted beneath a grid of Japanese tree lilacs. The stone path just outside her bedroom door leads to a working shower enclosed by an arching, interlacing circle of clipped hornbeam. It is her favorite garden feature. The shower, Mary boasts, is the exact proportions of the rotunda at the University of Virginia. "This one is leaky, but it has hot and cold running water. It's our tribute to Jefferson and Palladio." A waving line of boxwood separates the shower, the tree lilacs, and the plantings along the stone path from the open field. A short walk down into the high grass brings you to an oak tree and in its shade an old French iron bed, its fanciful headboard carved with twigs and vines and the figures of two deer looking longingly at each other. Mary discovered

Delicate blue flax (*Linum perenne*) seeds freely around the kitchen garden.

the bed at the New York Botanical Garden's yearly antiques show, and had it sent down to become an unexpected folly—"an outdoor guest room" in her garden. She has not decided yet whether to make a mattress of moss or one of turf, but intends to sleep there on a warm moonlit night. "I plan the garden to be enjoyed by us in an immediate and sensual way," she says.

Outside the kitchen, water spills gently from a sculpted stone of black granite in the center of a small terrace framed by four apple trees. Beds of culinary herbs such as sorrel, sage, fennel, basil, lemon balm, chives, and the thymes surround the terrace, combined with a cheerfully lavish display of flowers in bright primary colors. Sky-blue flax, yellow yarrow, blue hyssop, coreopsis, comfrey, alliums, dwarf yellow iris, orange poppies, red species lilies, and blue cornflowers are planted in billowing clumps. Persimmons, kerria, naked jasmine, clipped hard, and the chaste tree (*Vitex agnus-castus*) give weight and winter interest to the plantings.

Three of the beds are raised and edged with large old stones from the streets of Richmond. Some still have the yellow paint on them where

The kitchen garden is richly planted with herbs, perennials, bulbs, and shrubs in a yellow, scarlet, and blue color scheme. Cooking sage (*Salvia officinalis*), in profuse bloom, spills over stones salvaged from the streets of Richmond.

there were bus stops. Mary filled the beds first with gravel, then manure mixed with their native acid red clay. "The red clay here is very productive, but we amend it with a lot of horse manure." This is probably why her roses are flourishing, for they like a stiff, rich soil. Mary welcomes the challenge of gardening in the South, coming to grips with its heat and humidity. Mildew is inevitably a problem, but she discards any roses with foliage that can't stand up to the weather. She prunes back early blooming roses and perennials after their main flush in May and June, then waits for them to rally in the fall. "What's interesting in Virginia," she says, "is that you have several plant zones coming together. You can have lilacs, which need cold, and camellias. You have long languorous springs, then hot summers when it's really tropical, Zone 10, which is why the annuals do so well here. And then we have glorious autumns. The garden takes advantage of all those periods."

Around the kitchen garden and beyond it into the high grass are a number of birdhouses. Commissioned by Mary and Jamie, they were made locally, each carved to represent a place that would be necessary in a country village (Mary and Jamie made a list)—a post office, the church, a hardware store, the grain store, the veterinary clinic. If you stand quietly in Mary's gardens anywhere around the house, you are aware of birdsong. Bluebirds, indigo buntings, goldfinches, wrens, and cardinals abound. Jamie and Mary are certain they have so many birds because they have left all the land surrounding their house wild. "We have no lawn!" Mary exclaims proudly. The birds have the seed and fruit of Mary's planted shrubs and flowers, the high grass of the surrounding meadow, the water from the ponds, and the protection of the woods. Mary speaks passionately about "living in and with nature."

The apricot English rose 'Graham Thomas' flowers lavishly by the kitchen porch. Apple trees give structure to a terrace and the garden here, as do several birdhouses in the guise of village stores and a church.

The kitchen garden in late autumn is lit with the soft amber hues of the landscape.

"Our landscape is a natural one and a historical one. We have made it a personal one," Mary says. The house, the flowers in the garden, the very different places within the wild acreage, have become rich with personal associations. Mary speaks of the white iris she grows that Jamie loved from his aunt's place, Montpelier; she notes the pair of boxwood given them by their architect; the rose 'Little White Pet' that reminds her of a white dog she loved and lost named Toraighe. She mentions the tall oak trees on the knoll under which they built their house, and that in their library they have the original *Oaks of North America* in French with Redouté plates, which came with Jamie's ancestor E. I. du Pont to America, and has his bookplate. Once Jamie came to tell Mary there was a lily in bloom in the woods. "We went down and there it was, a single *Lilium superbum* in the ferns along the stream bank. It wasn't as vigorous as the ones tended in the garden but it thrilled me anyway. That is now the Lily Spot. When we want to reference where something is along that stream, we say 'above the Lily Spot' or 'below the Lily Spot.' It is personal to us, the reference to a natural event and to our witnessing of it and sharing it between ourselves." In this way, one's place becomes a personal narrative.

Mary is an intriguing combination of romantic, philosopher, and pragmatist. About their hunting, she says, "We've never lost a plant to deer. We manage the land for wildlife. We shoot the deer and then we eat them." (How sensible this seems! So many of our gardens are plagued by an overpopulation of deer, yet the venison we eat comes from New Zealand.) About her charming house that combines comfort with elegance, she says matter-of-factly, "This is a hunting lodge. It's meant to have dogs and thirty pairs of boots." About her garden and how it fits

IN THE SOUTHERN TRADITION

Hydrangeas hold their blooms into winter beneath a grid of Japanese lilacs.

into the landscape, however, she speaks eloquently: "I am not a native-plant fanatic but I am a lover of harmony. The fanciest cultivar in the garden often has its match wild in the landscape. The *Carpinus betulus* pruned into the shower rotunda is only a short distance from the *Carpinus caroliniana,* or ironwood, that arch over the riding trail near the beaver dam. The named cultivar of *Eupatorium* in the garden has its country cousin along the streams. When the *Cornus mas* is in bloom in the garden, we also see it in the woods and it is a sign to search for it and enjoy it there. The stream walk that is my favorite has delicate wisps of it along the upper banks, and I love to see it there and come home to see the massive pyramid of a specimen tree in bloom. Ferns and mosses edge the old confederate roads, which still have the tracks of wheels and horse ground into them, and these are also in the garden, intensified in their planting, a little more robust and cared for but echoing the spirit of the land." Mary speaks of the native blue lobelia that blooms in their woods and also in the garden. Here, "it is near its more sophisticated cousins with fancy names," she says, "but it has preceded them, and I know it will endure when they find a summer here too hot or too dry. The numerous plants of Chinese or Japanese origin that populate the garden share a common spirit with their Virginia cousins. They remind me of relatives at a Thanksgiving dinner; some things in common and enough differences to make it interesting."

RUTH KNOPF

Roses for Charleston

Charleston, South Carolina, that most picturesque small city, is known for its narrow eighteenth-century houses with high porches, or piazzas, along their sides to catch the sea breezes, and for its intimate, formal walled gardens. The city sits on a narrow peninsula shaped by the Ashley River on one side, and the Cooper River on the other, which, the saying goes, run together to form the Atlantic Ocean. The city and its surrounding countryside in what is called the Low Country is veined with many rivers and has glorious springs and falls, gentle winters and long, hot, humid subtropical summers. From the early eighteenth century until the Civil War, it was a prime cotton- and rice-growing area, and plantations along the rivers' edges, many recently restored, speak of its once great agrarian wealth.

Gardens flourished during this prosperity, and botanists and horticulturists were drawn to Charleston for its situation and its flora. Philadelphia nurseryman John Bartram and naturalist Mark Catesby came on visits to botanize. Eliza Lucas, who was born in Antigua and married Charles Pinckney in Charleston in 1744, introduced the cultivation of indigo, which became an important local crop for trade, as it was highly prized in Europe as a textile dye. Alexander Garden, a Charleston doctor and botanist, brought home South Africa's cape jasmine, which later became known as the gardenia in his honor. The great French botanist André Michaux came to collect plants, and introduced the first camellias here in 1786.

In 1802, John Champneys, a Charleston plantation owner, created America's first hybridized rose. He crossed the repeat-blooming

'Lamarque', a white Tea-Noisette dating from 1830, and 'Monsieur Tillier', a pink Tea created in 1891, flourish in a bed edged with 'Wintergreen' boxwood at Boone Hall.

'Dr. Rouges', a showy, rich-pink climbing Tea with quilled petals, is trained to a pillar at Boone Hall. Teas, Noisettes, and Chinas are the rose types Ruth Knopf finds most suitable to the subtropical climate of Charleston, South Carolina.

China rose (*Rosa chinensis* 'Old Blush'), which had recently arrived in America and Europe from the Orient, with the fragrant, clustered musk rose (*R. moschata*), first brought here by our colonists, resulting in what came to be known as 'Champney's Pink Cluster'. This he gave to his neighbor, Philippe Noisette, a Charleston nurseryman, who raised a new crop of roses from its seeds. In 1814, Philippe sent these new seedlings to his brother, nurseryman Louis Noisette, in Paris; eventually, one became known as 'Blush Noisette', and a new class of roses was established called Noisettes. The seedlings were later bred extensively with Tea roses, creating the climbing Tea-Noisettes.

The sweet-smelling, cluster-flowering Noisettes, and their relatives, the very fragrant nodding Chinas and Teas, were perfect roses for Charleston. Their ancestors came from the same latitude in China; they required no dormant period of cold, and bloomed almost continuously in the warm climate of South Carolina. They became favorites in the old Charleston gardens; but as new hybrids eclipsed the old, and big-flowered hybrid teas became the rage in the twentieth century, the original Chinas, Teas, and Noisettes disappeared, except in out-of-the-way places like cemeteries and old farmsteads. That is, until Ruth Knopf came along.

Ruth is South Carolina's champion of the old Southern roses, and is known and loved by rosarians everywhere from California to New Zealand. What began thirty years ago as a longing for these out-of-favor plants became an adventure, developed into a passion, and resulted in an expertise. "I started out looking for the five-petaled rose that I remembered from my childhood," Ruth says. It was one that grew in her South Carolina neighborhood when she was a child. "Someone told me it was a

IN THE SOUTHERN TRADITION

wild old rose." One summer, "when my children were little, we were at the beach for a week with my mother—in South Carolina, everyone goes to the beach in the summer—and she said, 'Here's five dollars, buy something for yourself.' On a table in a shop, there was a book called *Wild and Old Garden Roses* by Gordon Edwards. It was marked down to five dollars, so I bought it. I read it all winter."

At the time, Ruth lived with her family in a new house in Edgemoor, north of Charleston, where her husband was a minister. "There was nothing in the yard," she recalls. "I wanted to plant the things I liked." Ruth found a catalog of old roses from the California nursery Roses of Yesterday and Today, and ordered several plants from it. In the back of the catalog, she noticed a list suggesting books to read and an organization to join to learn about the old roses. The group was called Heritage Roses, and had a newsletter. One day after she joined, the group's editor Carl Cato, a fellow Southerner, called her. "He said he thought I should grow the old Tea roses because they would do so well. He recommended the nursery

A bed of pink Tea roses is underplanted with pinks grown from seed, the old-time, spicy-fragrant *Dianthus plumarius* 'Spring Beauty', in one of the garden beds at Boone Hall.

Thomasville Roses in Georgia—they carried a lot of them, and they were on their own roots." (Most nursery-grown roses are grafted, but ones grown on their own roots tend to be hardier and much longer lived.) "That's where I got my first Tea roses," Ruth says. I loved them. I've loved them ever since. I didn't know they got so big, but I had a lot of room where I lived. I had them everywhere, in the trees... My husband said, 'You've got to stop digging holes.' "

Ruth didn't buy all the roses she had read about and wanted, not only because of the expense, but because many were not available in nurseries. Fortuitously, she met the elderly rose collector Ruth Westwood who introduced her to the world of propagating roses from cuttings. She went to see Mrs. Westwood's garden of old roses in Newberry one Sunday when it was open. "I noticed a big bush with little blooms, and I asked her where to get it. She said you can't buy it, but you can root it. I told her I can't root it. I've never done that." Mrs. Westwood invited Ruth to return, promising to give her cuttings and teach her how to root them. "She had an old tin washtub up on bricks. She punched holes in the bottom and

LEFT: The fragrant ever-bloom-
ing Tea-Noisette 'Mme Alfred
Carrière' leans gracefully
against the iron fence border-
ing the street in Jane Waring's
Charleston garden.

BELOW: "You find it a lot in the
South," Ruth says of the great,
mounding chestnut rose, *R.
roxburghii.* Also called the burr
rose, prickles cover the buds
and the rose's thorns are
arranged backward.

filled it half and half with sand and peat moss. In the fall, she put her cuttings in; by spring they would be rooted." Ruth came home laden with slips of old roses—what are referred to among rose gardeners as "found" roses, not bought—to propagate and plant in her garden. As she became more experienced, she learned that she could root cuttings directly in the ground. "I dug a trench, added sand to the soil, and planted the cuttings, about six inches long, in rows one inch apart, setting them at an angle and covering them halfway with soil." This is the method she still uses today, taking rose stems that have just finished blooming, deadheading them, removing some of the leaves, and cutting just below a bud. (In colder climates, the same can be done by covering the cuttings with a glass jar to protect them from frost in winter.)

Since those early learning days, Ruth has tirelessly searched for the old roses in cemeteries, churchyards, and old-time gardens, identifying them, taking cuttings to root, growing them on, and nurturing them in her garden. She gathered other plants, too; the old-fashioned flowers and bulbs of the South, such as leucojums, the fragrant early daylilies, the

Ruth took cuttings of forgotten roses she found in old church yards, like the red Chinas here in the graveyard of the Unitarian Church in Charleston. "They're tough and long-lived," she says of the China roses.

spider lily (*Lycoris radiata*), and the varieties of *Narcissus*—the jonquills and tazettas—that survive the heat. (Most daffodils don't fare well in South Carolina because they need a cold period of dormancy.) The garden in Edgemoor was Ruth's canvas and her joy until her husband suddenly died in 1990. The church owned the house and asked her to leave. Ruth moved with her two daughters to Sullivan's Island, just east of Charleston, where they owned a small beach house. Shortly afterward, her Edgemoor garden was bulldozed. "It was so hard to leave that garden, because it was full of plants I found. All I did was plant things I liked. It was beautiful." Before she left, she sent off cuttings of her best-loved roses to fellow rosarians for safekeeping—nurserymen like Mike Shoup of the Antique Rose Emporium in Texas and Gregg Lowery of Vintage Gardens in California. She also brought babies in pots with her to Sullivan's Island. Many of those roses have since been planted all over Charleston.

Quietly, in her unassuming way, Ruth Knopf became a crusader. Having fallen in love with these old roses herself, she wanted to educate the people of Charleston to their beauty and good health, how preferable they were to the disease-ridden, fussy, spindly hybrid teas, favored in gardens, but more suitable for the show table. Ruth was involved with the International Heritage Roses Conference, which met every two years for tours and lectures in different parts of the world, but never on the East Coast. Backed by a committee of dedicated local gardeners, Ruth invited the group to come to Charleston for their meeting in 2001. "We wanted the conference to be educational," Ruth says, "so we decided to focus on the Noisette, because it was created here." Before the conference, Ruth was determined to replant the old historic roses in Charleston. "I thought it would be nice to do a trail of roses through the city." With the help of JoAnn Breland, the city horticulturalist, she designed the trail; Noisettes and Tea-Noisettes were planted at churches, meeting houses, museums, a hospital, on fences, in trees, from one end of Charleston to the other. A handy Heritage Rose Trail Map was published with a list of the roses at each location so that visitors might learn the flowers' names. Some listed were "found" roses with names, always in double quotation marks, that suggest their stories—"Mrs. Woods' Lavender-Pink Noisette," for instance, and "Pleasant Hill Cemetery."

In order to help identify the many Noisette hybrids, Ruth and JoAnn Breland felt they needed a garden where a complete collection of the roses could be grown side by side and compared, one that was "open to everyone for viewing and studying." JoAnn offered the garden beds (in the process of renovation) at the city's handsome old Hampton Park, where she worked. She and Ruth gathered an impressive collection of these roses, creating the Noisette Study Garden in time for the conference. Today, the old Charleston roses at the park have matured and continue to be studied using visual observations and DNA analysis for identification. And all over Charleston, the old vernacular roses are blooming once more. "At least we got the roses back

The globular, cream flowers of 'Mme Alfred Carrière' spill from a palm tree on King Street in Charleston. In 2001, a trail of old Noisette roses was established through the city, where the Noisettes were originally created.

White violas, white-flowering *Salvia superba*, and chamomile combine with the bold leaves of hymenocallis in a bed of white roses at Boone Hall. If kept deadheaded, the salvia will bloom indefinitely.

here," Ruth says modestly of her achievement. "It's so important. They're historic."

Ruth brought her favorite roses to other gardens in Charleston as well—private gardens she was asked to design. One garden, typically long and narrow and overlooked by the house's piazza, features a central brick path framed with China and Tea roses in rose, pink, and cream (among them, "Emmie Gray," Soncy," and "Spice") that were originally "found" roses in Bermuda and brought to Charleston. They are underplanted with blue violas in spring and white and blue wild lantana in summer. A small circular fountain spills water at the end of the path. At another garden, belonging to Ruth's friend Jane Waring, 'Mme Alfred Carrière', an elegant Tea-Noisette with fragrant cream flowers, arches high above an iron fence that borders the street. Single red poppies are scattered beneath. By the path to Jane's door, a pot bristles with a tiny white-flowered rose called "Cattail," a seedling named by Ruth from a rose she found on Cattail Road.

But the garden where Ruth has spent most of her energies in the last nine years, and where her talent as a garden designer excels, is at Boone Hall. Boone Hall is an old cotton plantation set on the Wampaugee Creek, a branch of the Cooper River a few miles northeast of Charleston. In 1995, Ruth was hired by the owner, Mrs. McRae. "She wanted roses. She was growing hybrid teas but they didn't do well for her, so she asked me to be her gardener." Boone Hall is privately owned but open to the public, and worth seeing on several counts. The house itself is relatively new, a 1935 attempt to replicate the original eighteenth-century farmhouse. A powerful sense of history, however, prevails in the entrance drive through a majestic allée of moss-draped live oaks planted in 1743, and a

long row of original brick slave quarters to one side of the drive is a forceful reminder of the underbelly of plantation life. But the best reason to visit Boone Hall is Ruth's garden by the house, an ambitious and gloriously executed planting in a pattern of generous curved beds ribboned with brick paths, enclosed by a box hedge.

In a way, Boone Hall replaced the garden Ruth had lost. She brought to its sun-filled beds her most treasured Chinas and Teas, Noisettes and species roses, knowing they would have the space and richness of soil here to flourish. She divided the symmetrical pattern of beds into pools of

In the warm-colored beds of the garden at Boone Hall, apricot roses are underplanted with Iceland poppies, bronze fennel, and the swordlike leaves of orange-flowering crocosmia.

An allée of live oaks, dripping with Spanish moss, lines the drive to Boone Hall. The oaks were planted in 1743 and, along with the brick slave quarters in their shadow, give a sense of plantation life.

colors, pale and rose pinks in view of the house, apricots and yellows beyond, whites to one side, then highlighted those color themes by underplanting the rose bushes with masses of one plant—spicy-smelling *Dianthus* 'Spring Beauty', white *Salviax suberba*, white oxalis, Johnny-jump-ups, wine-colored petunias, a tall chamomile, baby blue-eyes (*Nemophila menzieii*), gaudy orange Iceland poppies, and old crinum lilies. "I've put in here things that are typically grown in South Carolina," Ruth says, "and the roses are ones that I found." Ruth brought cuttings and seeds of annuals and perennials given to her by friends and propagated them in the plantation's nursery beds. And she let things seed around to get that unexpected lavishness that makes a garden so appealing. "I wanted it to be a real garden, like it would have been, full of plants given by people, a country garden." And she succeeded, for that is what makes this public garden astonishing. It is personal and unexpected in its sophistication and homeliness, in its splendid show and down-to-earth appropriateness. It reveals the loving eye and patience of a true gardener.

Ruth recently decided to give up the increasingly taxing job of caring for the Boone Hall garden. Her grown-up daughters persuaded her that it is time to put her energies into a garden of her own. Ruth's backyard in

Sullivan's Island is full of pots. Roses—hundreds of them, rooted from cuttings—are waiting to be planted. Other pots contain varieties of mock oranges, which she also collects, while others hold slips of treasures from friends. She hasn't had time to plant her garden, except for two borders of red China roses, carpeted with purple-and-white-striped morning glories ("the sort you see in Dutch botanical paintings") and fragrant pinks, on either side of the gravel walk from the street to her front porch. The soil here is much poorer, the climate hotter, and the terrible dollar weed causes mayhem in her beds. (A sign in her garden reads: "Free Weeds. Pull Your Own.")

But I have no doubt that she will make a magical garden here. And, as she does at Boone Hall when you slowly walk with her along the garden paths, she will tell you stories of where each plant was found, its provenance. "It has more meaning to you if you can't buy a plant, finding it instead, people sharing it with you. The plants mean more to you then. It's more than just a pretty garden. It's more than just landscaping."

Old-fashioned petunias, which reseed year after year, thread through a carpet of Johnny-jump-ups beneath the climbing rose 'Lady Waterlow'. Sometimes, Ruth says, "gardens do things on their own better than we can."

Texas Town and Country

I was amazed to learn that, in the ten distinct ecosystems found across the state of Texas, the average yearly rainfall ranges from eight inches—that is, desert-dry—in its most western regions, to a startling fifty-six inches along its lush eastern boundaries with Louisiana. Four of these different areas of vegetation—Blackland Prairie, Post Oak Savannah, South Texas Plains, and Edwards Plateau—come together in the middle of the state at San Antonio, the eclectic historic hub of south Texas, resulting in a rich diversity of plants, as well as birds and butterflies. The weather is mild here, with the threat of a freeze perhaps once every ten years, a gardener's Zone 8, and in protected spots, Zone 9a. Rain, averaging between twenty-four and twenty-eight inches a year, is erratic, with sudden heavy downpours in spring and again in hurricane season, often with dry periods in the heat of summer. San Antonio nonetheless, to my eye, boasts a verdant landscape, dominated by magnificent coastal live oaks (*Quercus virginiana*) that shade its residential streets with massive outstretched limbs, underplanted typically with ferns, ivy, and a lavish display of tropicals.

One hour's drive north from downtown San Antonio brings you to the heart of the Hill Country, specifically the Edwards Plateau, and a very different habitat—the still-wild, semiarid, rolling, hilly landscape beloved by Texas ranchers and farmers, and tourists in search of pastoral beauty. Here, too, evergreen live oaks set the scene, often solitary sculptures in the dry grasslands, picturesquely gnarled in the thin limestone soil. Post oaks and the plump, shrubby native rock cedar, *Juniperus ashei,* add their deep-green tones to the hills and pastures where peach orchards appear in satisfying rows.

A broad band of limestone cuts through the center of Texas, evidenced in both San Antonio and the Hill Country by the alkaline soil and the proliferation of creamy rough-textured limestone walls. Both regions have a warm climate, although the Hill Country is drier and cooler, temperate rather than subtropical. And both

Bold tropical plants flourish
in the residential gardens of San Antonio.

regions, interestingly, show a strong German influence, for these Europeans immigrated to San Antonio and the Hill Country by the thousands in the mid-to-late nineteenth century seeking a "new Germany." In the city, that influence, so evident in the gingerbread-laced Victorian architecture of the residential King William district downtown, was intertwined irrevocably with Spanish and Mexican aesthetics and culture. But in the Texas Hill Country, the German culture dominated the land and left a lasting legacy. Around Fredericksburg, in Gillespie County, their farms can still be glimpsed, self-contained within post-and-wire fencing or stacked limestone walls; and, in town, their charmingly prim, tiny Sunday houses of crumbling limestone and plaster still stand, merely one room above another, built so that they could spend Saturday night, then go to church the next morning before returning to the country. Wooden porches here are surrounded by filigree detail. Signs above the stores on Main Street still offer bratwurst and strudels. These transplanted Germans were skilled craftsmen in wood, stone, and iron, and they were great gardeners, toiling in their vegetable patches and orchards of fruit trees themselves, for they rarely used slaves. They were not only interested in fruit-and-vegetable culture but were keen botanists, and among the first settlers to enhance their homesteads with flowers such as old climbing roses loved in Europe and ornamentals in general.

The two gardens described here, one in Fredericksburg, the other in San Antonio, the work of landscape architect Sarah Westkaemper Lake, perfectly reflect their specific regions, and the differences and similarities they share.

Native Texan plants such as silver pony foot, *Dichondra argentea,* and blackfoot daisy, *Melampodium leucanthum,* spread in the crushed granite near the limestone tool house in Fredericksburg.

Limestone and Live Oaks

WITH TYPICAL ENTHUSIASM AND INSIGHT, Sarah Lake speaks of making gardens that reflect their specific settings not as a challenge but as "the fun of doing something so particular to itself." She likes the limitations of creating a garden based purely on an area's climate and ecology, its native vegetation, its history and culture, considering them "unifying constraints." And there are no settings with which she is more intimately familiar, more rooted in, than the Texas Hill Country and the region of San Antonio where she lives and where her family has lived for generations.

Sarah's maternal grandmother, Alta Meadows, was an Alamo siege descendent; more important, she was an avid plantsman and artist who recorded her deep interest in the native plants of her homeland by depicting them in hundreds of delicate botanical watercolors, some of which now line the staircase of Sarah's home. She was clearly a woman ahead of her time, interested in saving the native flora and in promoting it. "She was a wonderful mentor," Sarah says. So was one of Sarah's great-aunts, Sister Remberta Westkaemper, a nun who was also a botanist and created the prairie-grass herbarium for the state of Minnesota, where she lived. "I wasn't primarily interested in plants in those days," Sarah remembers of her teenage years and early twenties. "I was a flutist. But I visited my great-aunt annually, and she explained this concept of virgin prairie. She taught me how to find morels and to botanize. One time we were in the woods, and she said, 'I think we need a prayer,' and she lay down on her back in her habit, and I did too, looking up through the

Lombardy poplars, favored by the German settlers in Fredericksburg, but found nowhere else in Texas, are staged along the entrance drive in a meadow of sunflowers and snow-on-the-mountain (*Euphorbia marginata*).

ABOVE: A low limestone wall, recalling the German stacked stone fences, encloses the entrance courtyard of crushed Texas granite.

OPPOSITE: A gate opens from the courtyard to a narrow garden path behind the separate houses of the farm.

ferns and the trees. It was sublime." Perhaps, too, it was a pivotal moment. Sarah started her adult life as a professional musician, but by her mid-twenties decided that the world of music was too competitive, too introverted. She went back to school to get a degree in landscape architecture (from Louisiana State University). Gardens, she feels, are similar to music with their pattern of notes, their rhythms, and melodies. And a love of the land was in her blood. "Thinking about plants, growing, arranging, watching the countryside, was what everyone in my family did."

A favorite project that shows Sarah's skill and sensitivity as a plantsman and garden designer began three years ago when she was asked by San Antonio architect Don McDonald to do the landscape around Triple Creek Farm, which he was building as a weekend retreat on an old homestead in Fredericksburg. In the shade of a great umbrella-like pecan tree, the original small two-story house still stood, built by a well-to-do German farmer in the mid 1840s, now roofless and windowless, but with its thick walls intact, its crumbling limestone surface still showing vestiges of a pink-stained plaster. McDonald lovingly restored the little farmhouse cottage—it now serves as the owners' bedroom and sitting room—and then built a complex of complementary buildings around it that recall, in a clean, spare style, its distinctive vernacular. Three small identical "sister houses" of limestone and tide-water cypress, each with a bedroom and loft for the

LEFT AND RIGHT: The original nineteenth-century German homestead was restored by architect Don McDonald. He complemented the structure with three small limestone and cypress buildings, "sister houses," which provide bedroom quarters for the owners' three grown daughters. The buildings are separated from the orchard and fields by a limestone wall and arbor.

owners' three grown-up daughters, were built in line with the cottage, facing due south, and connected by a long porch. At right angles to the row of bedroom quarters, Don built a spacious two-story building he calls "the barn," which contains the family's living room, dining room, and kitchen, and creates an L-shaped compound. A high open porch, roofed in dusky red metal, runs the eastern length of the barn, ending in a tall stuccoed tower Don refers to as the spring house. From here, water spills from a spout, which could as well be shooting out grain, into a walled rectangular swimming pool he and Sarah designed to be reminiscent of a stock tank. "Everything," Sarah says, "was to look like an element from an Edwards Plateau sheep farm or cattle ranch rather than something suburban." A wood-and-limestone garage, a stone tool house, a small studio, and the original water-tank house with its windmill, restored at Sarah's urging, complete the complex.

It was Sarah's challenge to tie together all the different structures to make a whole. She wanted to design something practical for the weekend residents, who were eager to have an environmentally appropriate garden.

More important, she wanted it to be of the place, a garden that would speak of "the work ethic, the straight lines, and the orderly minimalism of the Germans." First, Sarah and Don collaborated on defining enclosed areas of the garden by connecting the buildings with low limestone walls built to recall the large pens the local German farmers made with stacked stone fences in their fields and around their vegetable gardens. The center open space of the compound is defined by such a wall, separating its grass lawn and pool from the hayfield and wild landscape beyond. Another wall runs behind the sister houses and original cottage to the tool house in the parking court, creating a narrow garden walkway shaded by a cedar "eye-brow" trellis. (An eyebrow trellis is really a shortened arbor with only one row of upright supports and short crosspieces jutting out like eyebrows.) A third wall connects the barn with the garage on one side, and the tool house and the first of the sister houses on the other, creating a large park-ing court that serves as an entrance to the farm.

The approach to the farm is along a curving drive of crushed Texas granite that wends through a grassy grove of live oaks, and then through a

Light in the Texas summer can be excruciating, so arbors and trees are important to Sarah's design. The garden path is shaded from the hottest sun by the row of houses, a limestone wall, and an eyebrow trellis of peeled cedar.

meadow of wildflowers, where the intriguing complex of buildings that make up the farm can first be seen. Although Sarah added live oaks to those already existing along the drive, she says oaks that are planted never have the picturesque branching pattern, implying stress and age, that the native ones display. She planted a drift of Lombardy poplars to "push the drive into place" as it curves through the meadow in front of the farm. The poplars "add sequence and motion," with their poetic, vertical outlines, and are historically appropriate, for they were used and cherished here by the German settlers in the late nineteenth century, but appeared nowhere else in Texas.

Through a gateway, merely a pair of high posts and a crossbar made of peeled cedar, is the walled courtyard. The planting within the parking court, which is dressed with crushed local pink Texas granite, is strikingly simple. Gray-leaved silver pony foot (*Dichondra argentea*), the white-flowering blackfoot daisy (*Melampodium leucanthum*), *Gaura lindheimeri* (named for the German botanist Ferdinand Lindheimer, who settled here), and lavender are planted in repeated drifts along the base of the surrounding stone wall. All are Texas Edwards Plateau natives, except the lavender, which Sarah felt comfortable including because it is an agricultural crop in the Hill Country. Sarah has allowed this fringe of low-growing perennials to spread unhampered ("sometimes you can plant something and let it alone"), and the resulting pools of gray foliage and white flowers against the pink of the gravel and the creamy walls are understated and pleasingly effective. Confederate jasmine spills out of a terra-cotta pot by the entrance steps, and the climbing rose 'Old Blush', a favorite of the early Germans, twines around a trellis by an old water-filled trough against the tool house. Cross-vine (*Bignonia capreolata*) runs along the eaves of the barnlike garage. Sarah planted a native red oak, *Quercus shumardii,* in the center of this large graveled court, which in its large and broad mature state will provide welcome shade and appropriately scaled structure.

Within the compound, outside the sister houses and main living barn and around the pool, Sarah kept the garden quite plain, merely a row of cedar elms hugging the daughters' long porch, and a flat plane of green reaching to the low stacked walls that divide the garden from the hay field beyond. The owners wanted a lawn, but there was not enough water for a velvety sward; instead, they planted baby Bermuda grass, a dwarf hybrid that tolerates drought by going dormant and then reviving with rain. In the protected, shadowy microclimates of the narrow alleys between each of the sister houses and the original cottage, and along their western backs, Sarah created walking paths with stones and crushed granite, and then planted their edges with Texas natives that would thrive without cosseting. Creeping violets (*Viola missouriensis* and *V. hederacea*), yellow columbines (*Aquilegia hinckleyana*), purple wine cups (*Callirhoë involucratae*), pigeon berry, white ruellia, river fern, water clover, lycoris, and salvias add color and texture much of the year. The eyebrow trellis of peeled cedar, partially covered already with old rambling roses and yellow trumpet vine, provides shade from the harsh Western light along the garden alleyway behind the houses. Just behind the trellis, the limestone wall visually divides the narrow garden from an orchard and vegetable garden beyond it. Here, in a field of native buffalo grass, Sarah planted an orchard of Mexican plum trees (*Prunus*

The thin, limey ground beneath the arbor is planted with native yellow columbines (*Aquilegia hinckleyana*), river ferns, white ruella, salvias, and purple wine cups (*Callirhoë involucrata*). "Native plants don't need intravenous feedings," Sarah says.

A towerlike spring house juts out from the two-story barn that houses the family's living room, dining room, and kitchen. Water shoots from a spout into the raised swimming pool Sarah and Don designed to resemble a stock tank.

mexicana, indigenous to the Edwards Plateau) around a circular vegetable patch the owners requested. The plums in the orchard are still too young to make much of an effect, but old specimens in Fredericksburg are picturesque in outline with beautiful banded bark. "Beige-pink flowers that smell of jasmine tea" in spring are followed by "incredible little purple and yellow fruit." Beneath the trees, Sarah planted oxblood lilies (*Rhodophiala bifida*) in a diamond pattern in the grass. (I was charmed by another name for these scarlet amaryllis-like bulbs—"schoolhouse lilies," because they bloom when it's time to go back to school.) "Their green leaves come out after they bloom, in winter, defining the pattern in the grass, which is a buff color then." Sarah says she was trying to suggest that there was a garden here before the new complex of houses was built. "The appearance of bulbs where old homesteads were I find very moving."

Sarah loves the rough grass of the Hill Country. She loves the color and the leafy, pungent smell of the fields. And there is a continuity to this countryside that she treasures, a consistency caused by the thin, rocky soil and limited groundwater. "The climate here," she says, "the difficulties of gardening, limit the possibilities of excess, so the community gets a restrained and uniform appearance." This restraint at the Fredericksburg farm, the spare beauty of the landscape, and the architecture as well, is outstanding.

Sarah does quite a bit of design work on ranches in the Edwards Plateau ("the rural work is really my favorite"), but the Fredericksburg

garden she singles out as a dream project, due to a harmonious collaboration with the client and architect, as well as the challenge of the site. "Because of the low rainfall, and the exposure here, the planting will always have an austere quality," which Sarah feels is as it should be. "I like projects with water restrictions" she continues. "I have a better chance of having open space—negative space; the silences are clearly perceived. Maybe this comes from a musical background."

Beyond the low limestone wall, hay fields bleed into the natural Hill Country landscape.

BELOW AND OPPOSITE: The San
Antonio garden of architect
Ted Flato is planted with large
bold-leaved tropicals that
stand up to the power of the
oaks and strong presence of
the Spanish-inspired Arts and
Crafts house.

When Sarah describes Ted Flato's very different garden on four-tenths of
an acre in the Alamo Heights neighborhood of San Antonio, she also
thinks in musical terms—of rhythm, balance, and sequence. This, however, is a garden that throws austerity to the wind. Ted Flato, along with
Sarah's former husband, David Lake, heads up the acclaimed architectural
firm Lake-Flato, known for its environmentally sensitive, energy-conserv-
ing, innovative designs in Texas and elsewhere. He lives with his wife,
Katy, and two daughters in a large, comfortable, rather quirky house, built
in 1909, which Sarah calls "an eclectic, eccentric Moorish-Mediterranean
enclave." The house, rough-surfaced stucco painted a dusky orange with
yellow wood trim, and the enclosed, very private garden with its shaded
patios, luxuriously planted with hardy tropicals and featuring water and
rustic stonework, perfectly reflects the distinctive San Antonio-Hispanic
idiom. That style, Sarah says, historically included "flamboyant, exotic
plants in an enclosed area, abundant water as ornament, strong color, pattern, and hand-built, colored concrete or stone veneer masonry elements,
showing the artisan's hand. Entertaining, and outdoor gathering for pleasure," she adds, "was very much a part of life."

The Flatos' garden is the result of a collaboration between Sarah and
Ted started seven years ago, when Sarah was called in to "connect the
dots"—that is, unify the various parts into a whole with plantings and
paths. The small corner-lot property is dominated by two extraordinary
live oaks several hundred years old. Their massive, writhing branches
reach up and out over the garden, filtering its light and giving it a powerful sense of drama. Native river ferns and holly ferns, chosen for their
coarse foliage, now clothe the ground beneath the oaks, and fan palms,

bananas, gingers, and elephant ears ("plants loved in San Antonio for generations") explode in luxuriant profusion around the trees and along the perimeters of the garden, giving it complete privacy. The exaggerated, architectural boldness of these large-leaved plants, Sarah knew, would effectively balance the power of the trees, as well as the strong presence of the house.

From the street, you catch only a glimpse of this dramatic, shadowy interior garden through a pair of iron gates and an arbor smothered in Mexican butterfly vine (*Mascagnia macroptera*) and cross-vine. On either side of the gate piers, Sarah planted a billowing thicketlike hedge of sun-loving South Texas natives—fine-textured, thorny, and vividly colored plants. Mexican honeysuckle (*Dicliptera suberecta*), esperanza, *Salvia regla*, Copper Canyon daisies (*Tagetes limmerii*), agaves, and caesalpinias tangle together—a mass of silver foliage and red, orange, and yellow blossoms, "all hummingbird attracters." Between the hedge and the curb, Sarah finished off with a border of prairie buffalo grass. "Most people would think this needs to be reported to the authorities," she says, bemused at the rather unkempt, deliberately wild effect of the street planting. "It's an attempt to celebrate the wonderful textures of the brush country." And it satisfied Ted's desire for a sustainable planting as well as Katy's desire for color and flowers. "The idea was to come through the thorny brush to the big-leaved interior," Sarah says, enjoying the contrast between the entry garden's more delicate "foamy" appearance, its pale foliage and bright flowers, with the darker drama, "the brutality," inside.

Ted and Sarah changed the front entrance to the house, returning it to a Moorish-detailed side door, with arching glass panels and painted yellow

Prairie buffalo grass edges the curb in front of a wild planting of south Texas natives.

wood, which Ted thinks was the original front door. From the iron gates off the street, they laid a broad path of stained concrete squares through the first level of the garden to the new entrance. "Our idea," Ted says, "was to use the garden as our entry hall." Walls of rough-surfaced stucco, the same melony color as the house, mark a broad landing Sarah designed at the entrance. From there, in a continuous axis from the front gates, a series of stone steps and a gravel path lead down through the garden and into what Ted calls its rooms. "It's not all jungle," Sarah remarks, referring to the densely luxurious plantings of exotics and Texas natives. "The garden has some defended voids." Two generous clearings, one stone-surfaced, the other graveled, offer seating in the shade of the vast, ivy-clad oak trees. In the final patio, a pleasing oval enclosed originally with a

The thick, thorny, colorful plants of the brush country were planted by Sarah along the street entrance of the Flatos' garden as a contrast to the big-leafed interior garden.

colonnade of Texas palms, and now curtained with bamboos, Ted had a fanciful fountain made of honeycomb rock from the Edwards Plateau, which is bursting with native maidenhair ferns. It is a typical folly of old San Antonio gardens. Another piece of garden sculpture, a concrete bench carved to look like a log, is an example of an extraordinary vernacular art form in downtown San Antonio. It is locally called "rustico" work, and was created by Mexicans starting in the early twentieth century. Arbors, railings, bus stops, and seats along the city streets and in the parks are seemingly rustic log work, fashioned out of concrete—what in Europe is called "faux bois."

Ted preserved vestiges of the garden that predate his ownership. Old boxwood hedges remain, and pittosporum, ivy that climbs into the tree limbs, and even an old cyclone fence between the garden and the street. "Cyclone fences were born in Dallas in the 1940s and 1950s," Sarah says. "Ted loved it and didn't want to change it. Ted and Katy cherish the off-hand and the awkward in things. Anything with a little bit of character, Ted always protects."

When Ted and Katy bought the property eight years ago, the driveway wrapped around the back of the house and ended in a parking area. Hating to see land wasted, Ted shortened the driveway, ending it on the far side of the house where the visitor is unaware of its existence. The old parking area eventually became the oval patio with the honeycomb fountain. At the back of the house, he built a garage, and above it, an open-air pavilion that extends off the kitchen. "The pavilion allows you to get out in the garden," Ted says; it is the connection between inside and out. Here, through the limbs of the oak trees, the garden can be seen in its

Honeycomb rock from the Edwards Plateau was used to encrust a fountain now spouting ferns as well as water—a centerpiece of one of the terraces and a typical San Antonio folly.

entirety, with its spiky palms and bronze-leaved bananas, its pots and stone patios, benches and fountain.

    The atmosphere of the Flato garden, the combination of its various elements brings to mind the Sunken Garden in San Antonio's Bracken-ridge Park, a spot Sarah frequents with enthusiasm. From a Japanese-style roofed archway of concrete "rustico" work, steps lead up to a marvelously eccentric circular stone pavilion, made with stacked stone pillars and thatched with palm leaves. From here, you look down into a garden of exotic plants, many from South America, that are staged around the sides of an old quarry, its pools filled with water until recently. Walking paths of rough limestone wind around its edges. The top of the quarry is rimmed with a tangle of wild native shrubbery. The Sunken Garden, originally

Sarah and Ted chose coarse-textured native river and holly ferns and a fan palm—"exaggerated, almost architectural" plants—to complement the drama of the great oak trees.

Ted added a pavilion off the kitchen of his family's house to overlook the lush tropical garden Sarah and he created. A cement bench, disguised as wood, is typical of the "rustico" work found all over San Antonio.

(and now officially again) called the Japanese Tea Garden, was conceived by a city parks commissioner in 1917 and built in part by prison labor at an old Portland cement quarry. The intent was to create a Japanese garden. Indeed, plants were brought from Asia, and in the 1930s, a Japanese couple lived there, tended the garden, and served tea to crowds of visitors—until Pearl Harbor, when they were evicted. Sarah fell in love with this magical place when she was a child, for she was taken there often by her grandmother "who would perch herself on a bench and just let us play around the stone walks curving up and down and around the quarry." The adventure of the Sunken Garden, its fantasy, its plantings of tropicals and wild rim of native vegetation, its stonework and water, all remain a strong influence in Sarah's San Antonio garden designs and were a basis of her vision for the Flatos.

Sarah says she likes to emphasize "the idea of time" in a garden; that is, a sense of age. References, in the use of plants and materials, to the region's history and tradition achieve this; so does the preserving of old elements (the boxwood and cyclone fence at the Flatos', the pump house and cottage at Fredericksburg), and allowing the vernacular plantings a certain freedom. "In the Fredericksburg garden, which is new, I wanted it to seem as if the plants had been left alone for a period of years." Similarly, a certain look of dishevelment is preferred by Sarah and Ted in the Flato garden, a relaxed show of age. In both gardens, the plants are not highly manipulated, Sarah says. "When you're creating something, you don't want to intervene too much." (We all know how nature, left alone, can miraculously relax a garden design, blurring its edges, weaving its parts into a whole.)

Sarah's approach to gardening is more intellectual than spontaneous. Many of us garden purely for the love of it, to grow and weed and muck about in the soil, without thinking too much about the "why" of what we're doing. The idea, the theme of our gardens, if there is one, often evolves almost by happenstance. But, perhaps because Sarah is an especially thoughtful, introspective person, her gardens are driven by ideas. Those ideas are rooted deeply in her knowledge of the local character, history, and ecology of the regions where she works. And so, remarkably, the gardens she makes—spare and farmlike in Fredericksburg, voluptuous and quirky in Alamo Heights—do not reflect her so much as they reflect the place where they are. The more attuned a gardener is to the site, its climate, and traditions, Sarah feels, the more opportunity there is for originality in the garden's design.

Exuberant, eclectic mixtures of plants that include bananas and other tropicals are the vernacular style in the gardens of Alamo Heights.

The California Garden

Dick Turner, plantsman and editor of the splendid periodical *Pacific Horticulture,* once described the quintessential California garden to me as wall-enclosed, with a pool, arranged for outdoor living, and dressed with plants that thrive in the hot, dry climate. Walled patios and courtyards are an indelible part of California's history, introduced as a style by the Spanish missionaries in the late eighteenth century. Twenty-one missions were built, each a day's journey apart, along the Pacific coast between San Diego and Sonoma. They were walled and planted with olive trees and orchards, and always contained a courtyard around a fountain or well. The padres' idea of the enclosed courtyard harked back to southern Spain, with its Moorish—and fundamentally Persian—aesthetic. The wells and fountains in the California missions were not only practical, they were a symbolic honoring of water, as they were in the gardens of Spain and in ancient Persia, suggesting an oasis in an arid landscape.

The old abandoned missions continue to inform California garden design today. The plants that have survived without irrigation—the aloes, agaves, and olives—are noted and revered for their ruggedness, and the enclosed colonnaded courtyards and fountains themselves inspire our notions of outdoor living in a hot climate. California garden designers Nancy Goslee Power and Bernard Trainor are certainly influenced by this old vernacular style. They take the idea of enclosure, the courtyard, the walls, the pools of water, and reinterpret them in a contemporary way. Two of the four landscapes in the following pages are examples of the quintessential California walled garden; the other two reach out beyond their walls to embrace the stunningly beautiful natural setting of evergreen oaks and dry golden hills.

A very private and colorful garden in Santa Monica
is hidden behind a high masonry wall painted bright yellow.

BERNARD TRAINOR

Planting in Gravel

It is perhaps an irony that one of the great champions of sustainable gardening in California is a native not of the state, but of Australia. Landscape designer Bernard Trainor feels quite at home in his new land— after all, he has traded one rugged coast for another, and the climates and plant palettes are similar. He is passionate about the need to use plants in the gardens he designs south of San Francisco that will thrive on their own in the dry, hot weather that persists from May to October. "There's not enough water here," he says, "and I want to do landscapes that are ecologically sound and appropriate to their context." Bernard thinks of himself as a plantsman, but he is just as much an artist, for his landscapes of native grasses, shrubs and trees, succulents, and Mediterranean herbs are stunningly beautiful.

"My whole background is plants," he says. Bernard's first horticultural experience was his five years as an apprentice gardener in Australia, "mostly doing things I detest—maintaining water-guzzling lawns and planting 'Victorian' color schemes with 'look-at-me' annuals." The good result was that being involved in the management of those gardens made him aware of how wrong that sort of planting was for the environment in which he was working. Happily, as the leading apprentice, he was awarded a scholarship to study landscape design at Chelsea Physic Garden in London. He left for England in 1989 and, before starting the program at Chelsea, landed a temporary job working for Beth Chatto. "I knew this was the place for me," he recalls, referring to Chatto's then-innovative approach to creating gardens

The hardscaping around the raised swimming pool in Palo Alto was softened with a bold mixture of drought-tolerant herbs, succulents, and grasses planted in the graveled ground.

A striking *Phormium cookianum* repeats the lines of the iron grill gate at the entrance to Andrea and Andy Vought's house.

in tune with their specific habitats. She reinforced what Bernard realized was crucial in garden design—learning the workings of nature. "She taught you to *look* at nature," he says. Bernard was fortunate enough to be with Chatto while she was making her now-famous gravel garden. Gravel would become an essential feature in his garden designs in California. "She had a huge impact on my work," he says. So did Derek Jarman's poignant, thought-provoking garden of plants and found objects in the stone and shale on the coast of Dungeness, England.

By 1994, Bernard was practicing as a garden designer in England and traveling "incessantly, devouring gardens in search of direction and inspiration." In 1995, an ad in *Gardens Illustrated*, for a position as garden manager and designer at a property in the Bay area of California, caught his attention. He came, worked there for a year, then started his own design business and settled on the coast of Monterey.

In 1999, Andrea and Andy Vought asked Bernard to design them a garden in Palo Alto. Bernard thinks of it as one of his first "really liberating projects," since the Voughts allowed him free rein to experiment on their property. They had just finished renovating the one-story house they had bought a few years earlier, adding on a bedroom wing to what had originally been a tract house built in the 1950s. Although situated on a closely populated residential street in the middle of urban Palo Alto, the

house sat on a deep corner lot, one-half acre in size, with a creek behind it. When they bought it, the front of the house, Andrea recalls, was dressed up with azaleas and camellias. There were no plantings in the rest of the yard—just a sand pit for kids, a swing set and a hot tub. The back of the property onto which the new bedroom wing opened was virtually inaccessible, thickly populated with thirteen huge, shaggy eucalyptus trees. Andrea wanted an outdoor living space—so essential in California—and a garden to look out on and enjoy. She had recently seen some of Bernard's work on a local garden tour and knew immediately he was the one to design their small property. Impressed with his artistry, she also cared, as he did,

Olive trees, so tolerant of the arid California summers, shield the Voughts' house in Palo Alto from the street. Purple teucrium, sage, stachys, and euphorbias carpet the gravel along the entrance steps.

Aloes and agaves, the old vernacular plants of the Spanish missions, perfectly survive the summer heat and drought.

about being ecologically responsible. Over the next year, Bernard transformed the flat, dreary yard with masonry walls and steps, then covered the rest of the ground with gravel and planted in it a tapestry of native shrubs, perennials, and drought-resistant Mediterranean plants.

The plantings distinguish the house on the street. Most of the other front yards could be in Fairfield, Connecticut, so lush are their green lawns and clipped evergreens, their hybrid tea roses. (Almost anything can be coaxed to grow in California with enough irrigation.) The Voughts' front yard, in contrast, is planted with olive trees in gravel. Silvery sage, stachys, teucrium, *Euphorbia rigida*, and Santa Barbara daisies (*Erigeron karvinskianus*) carpet the ground along the broad stone steps that lead to the front door, creating a quiet lushness that seems at home in their arid California setting.

Their half acre is secluded, surrounded on all sides by a high wooden fence. Not a stitch of lawn remains, nor the azaleas and the invasive eucalyptus. In their place are native red-stemmed manzanita, madrone (*Arbutus menziesii*), a strawberry tree (*A. unedo*), and several *A.* 'Marina' with bright orange berries and flowers the hummingbirds love. Voluptuous phormiums, agaves, aloes, euphorbias, and succulents—all of which thrive in gravel through the summer heat—make dramatic pictures of color and texture. Bernard speaks of aloes and agaves as "the old fuddy-duddy plants in the missions out here. They're the survivors. You go to old abandoned missions (or old farmhouses in Australia) to see what is still there. These are the classic vernacular plants." The plants might be old-fashioned, but they are visually striking and seem very modern with Bernard's handling.

Phormiums, aeoniums, graptoverias, and grasses, along
with aloes and agaves, form a
rich tapestry around the pool.

Before Bernard introduced plants to the Voughts' gravel garden, however, he had to establish a structure—bones that would give the garden
year-round character. Andrea and Andy wanted a swimming pool, and the
only place where one would fit was the backyard outside the master bedroom wing. The land here was flat, and the house was low in profile, but a
grove of remaining eucalyptus trees beyond the property line towered
above the boundary fence. Bernard felt that in order to make the transition between the low land and the tall trees, they needed to introduce
some height. Just outside the house he built a terrace and a bocce court
beneath a steel-and-masonry pergola. From there he raised the level of the
ground with masonry retaining walls and sited the pool on this higher elevation up a series of steps. It is a brilliant feat, for you look across the
water at eye level from the terrace and house, and it appears like a sliver of
mirror reflecting light. Behind the pool, Bernard built three high, free-
floating masonry walls, curving two of them. He treated them almost like
sculptures, and used them as backdrops for his plantings. "The standing

A bronze-and-steel sculpture by Frank Morbillo stands between two free-standing sections of wall and is echoed in color by dark *Aeonium arboreum* 'Schwarzkopf'.

walls were scary-looking at first without any plants," Andrea says. Their yard, yet unplanted, seemed an expensive expanse of gravel.

"Trust me," Bernard said. He rewarded their faith with an astonishingly rich and painterly display of plants that brought their walls and ground to life. The smooth walls, stained a taupe, now perfectly set off the agaves, aeoniums, graptoverias, aloes, stachys, phormiums and grasses that Bernard plays against them with such skill. He repeats a gorgeous color range from glaucous blue to lettuce green to rust red to faded pinky green to chartreuse with their different foliage.

Along both sides of the bocce court, herbs provide various shades of green and gray—thymes, purple sage, yarrow, santolina, germander, fennel, and lemon balm—all tolerant of summer heat and drought. Andrea cuts the herbs back after their first flush of growth and bloom in May to renew them for the long months to come. "The long growing season can wear plants out," Bernard says. "They don't know when to stop. The salvias and yarrows never stop growing, so you have to cut them back. But the aloes and agaves don't get worn out." Bernard uses his favorite vernacular plants throughout the garden, from the front gate past the kitchen courtyard to the back pool area. Phormiums also add bold spiky foliage here to contrast with smoky purple fennel, orange-flowering kangaroo paws and countless varieties of euphorbias (*E. robbiae, rigida, wulfenii, griffithii* 'Fireglow', and *E. myrsinites*). By the kitchen, a barbe-cue and outdoor dining table and chairs are at the ready in what the Voughts call their eatable garden where borders of culinary herbs (borage, sage, oregano, rosemary, scented geraniums, basil) grow in the gravel by the house walls. A large terra-cotta-colored jar, centered at the far end of this area, is filled with water, which gently overflows onto the gravel, and is then recirculated. Planted around it are *Aloe saponaria*, the blue-leaved *Euphorbia rigida*, a coral-pink flowering stachys, and purple fennel. The soil was enriched before being covered with gravel in areas of the garden where plants are clustered. Along the walking paths, the gravel covers a layer of fabric cloth over subsoil. With time, the plants seed and blur the definitions.

"I've always been a gravel fanatic," Bernard says. "I grew up with it. It's still a dirty word here in California, but it's an inexpensive, honest material. The great thing about gravel is that water goes back into the land. So many surfaces of hardscaping don't absorb water." And lawns! Bernard sees the unnaturalness, the inappropriateness of green lawns in a state that has, in the summer and fall, a stunningly beautiful native land-scape of dark evergreen oaks on golden hillsides. "So many people want *green* here. They bring that baggage with them." He laments that people buy plots of land with the majestic valley or coastal oaks—California's most splendid trees—but decide they don't like the look of the sere, warm beige grasses that color the ground from June to November. So they put in lawns and an irrigation system, not realizing that those prize oaks will die. The oaks don't like water in summer, Bernard says—they can't take water twelve months of the year without deadly funguses developing.

A graceful pot from the Maine company Lunaform serves as a gentle water feature. The glau-cous blue *Euphorbia rigida*, *Aloe saponaria*, and orange-flowering kangaroo paws spread in the gravel at its base. Purple cotinus smokes in the background.

Rosemary 'Tuscan Blue' and
Euphorbia rigida border the
path to the pool at the Moores'
garden in Los Altos Hills.

In Los Altos Hills, in a gated community rife with green lawns and oaks that are therefore dying, Bernard designed a stunning dry garden for Marie and Geoff Moore. On a hillock between the one-story house and the road, he underplanted a magnificent valley oak (*Quercus lobata*) with native California grasses. When the grasses turn golden in summer, Marie told me, neighbors (not connecting with the native landscape) come by to point out to her that the grasses she and her husband had so painstakingly planted beneath the trees are dead.

Bernard calls the Moores' property his best urban garden. "Urban" is a relative term. My New York eye would call this an exurban—or at most a suburban—garden, for it encompasses one acre and has a borrowed view of olive trees, pines, and distant blue hills. It is brilliantly designed. More minimal than the Vought garden in Palo Alto, it shows off Bernard's fine-honed skill in combining walls, water, and drought-loving plants in gravel. From the driveway the garden entrance is through an iron gate Bernard designed, similar to the Voughts'. But here it leads immediately to the back of the property, behind the house where a stone and gravel path leads to a narrow swimming pool. The path, in full sun, is softened on both sides with spilling dark-green rosemary 'Tuscan Blue' and the beautiful glaucous blue *Euphorbia rigida.* Creeping thymes weave among the stones. Three small olive trees are planted in the corners. A large purple-hued concrete pot of *Kalanchoe beharensis* and the fescue 'Siskiyou Blue' marks the entrance to the pool. The pool is V-shape, following the property's setback, and is starkly delineated. Two floating four-foot-high masonry walls border its ends, and a low, slatted wood fence divides its long side from the wild countryside beyond. Between the wood fence and the pool, Bernard planted a two-foot hedge

Native California grasses border the street in front of the glorious valley oak (*Quercus lobata*) that marks the entrance to the property.

The back terrace is shaded by three Chinese elms planted in the 1950s by Thomas Church. Bernard added a low curved concrete wall and circular vase of spilling water, and planted the surrounding gravel with bronze phormiums and euphorbias.

of dwarf olive (*Olea* 'Little Ollie'), and, behind it, tall spikes of restio, *Thamnochortus insignis.* A simple pipe spills water from here into the pool.

Broad steps lead up from the pool through another iron gate to the back terrace, bringing you from brilliant sun to dappled shade. The terrace is shaded by three handsome Chinese elm trees, which were planted in the 1950s by the great landscape architect Thomas Church, and are all that remains of his design. To define this terrace and delicately separate it from the wild landscape of olives and pines beyond it, Bernard again employed his dramatic free-standing walls—in this case, only three feet tall and beautifully curved, one part concave, the other joining it, convex. They are stained a soft gray brushed with brown, which is echoed in the color of the pebbles on the ground and the elm tree trunks of gray bark peeling to reddish orange. The walls serve as seating and embrace a round, concrete bowl of water spilling softly into the gravel. On either side of the walls and around the terrace, chartreuse-flowered spurges, *Euphorbia robbiae* and *E.* 'Portuguese Velvet', are repeated in the gravel and contrasted with clumps of dark bronze-leaved phormiums, green aeoniums, and delicate beige-pink-green grasses. Phormiums by themselves border the walls of the house. The living room and dining room of the

attractive, unpretentious house open through a long hallway down broad concrete steps onto this most pleasant shadowy gravel terrace.

From the opposite north-facing windows of the dining room, a Barragá-nesque view is framed in a large-paned picture window of the front garden with its red-stemmed madrones (the beautiful variety *Arbutus* 'Marina') and fabulous oak tree. The ground slopes toward the house, and Bernard added boulders of Napa fieldstone to hold back the elevation and provide room for a stone path around the house. Then he carpeted this south-facing slope with madrones and fifteen hundred native bunch grasses—*Carex tumulicola*, the Berkeley sedge that does well in sun or shade, California rush (*Juncus*), and *Stipa arundinacea*, which turns a lovely orange in the dry season. By the front entrance of the house, which is in deep shade, he staged the upright, evergreen South African restio, which grows to nine feet.

Marie and Geoff remodeled the house to have an Asian flavor, opening out to the garden on all sides. They are thrilled with what Bernard has created. "There is always something to discover and delight in," Marie says. "It has become a calming source in our life, a living mantra."

A hedge of dwarf olive, *Olea* 'Little Ollie', vertical spears of restio, *Thamnochortus insignis*, and a slatted wooden fence mark the boundary between the pool and wild landscape beyond.

In Carmel Valley, Bernard had the opportunity to work on a much larger scale—eleven acres of ravishing countryside. His clients, the Ryleys, bought this generous parcel of land in a newly developed community where large houses and lawns were being installed. They, on the contrary, built a complex of modest structures from which to look out on a view they loved—gently rolling meadow and woodland clothed with coastal live oaks, buckeyes, and native grasses. During construction, the land along the Ryleys' long, curving driveway was scraped of vegetation and no more than a bare construction site was left around the new buildings. Bernard's job was to create outdoor living spaces, restore this land, and connect it seamlessly with the natural landscape.

First Bernard replanted the verges of the drive to the house with native flowers and fescues. Monkey flowers and bush lupines, ceanothus,

A series of platforms was designed around outbuildings and the house from which to view the landscape of native oaks, "so that we're the observers," Bernard says.

and deer grass (*Muhlenbergia rigens*) now carpet the roadside. He "pulled the woodland down to the driveway" by planting more oaks along its edges. Around the small guest house, which is the first building you come to, Bernard built a stone terrace and then established a meadow of yarrow, California poppies, and deer grass as a foreground to the view of fields and oaks. A bold-leafed grape, *Vitis californica* 'Roger's Red', clothes the side of the green-stained wooden structure. Farther along the gravel drive are more outbuildings—a studio and barn, all painted a deep green so that they disappear in the landscape. Bernard designed a simple wooden terrace off the studio that surrounds one of the beautiful lichen-covered oaks. A low stone wall frames the terrace where he placed a small square concrete reflecting pool, edged with pebbles. The driveway ends on a hilltop at the spare main residence, which looks out onto the magnificent scenery. Again, a stone-framed terrace extends from the house; on the slope below it, thousands of native fescues were established. The terraces built around the guest house, studio, and main house are like a series of platforms, Bernard says, from which to view nature.

At a site like this, he feels "you can't turn your back on the powerful view, or ignore what's around you. As a designer, half your job is figuring out how *not* to get in the way." The result here of Bernard's sensitive creativity, of course, is that, except for the spare stone walls and terraces, no

garden is apparent. "It's a minimalist, underdone landscape," he says. In fact, "simple is harder to do than fancy. I learned so much on this property," he says. "It was pivotal. You observe, then you plant, and sit back and hope for the best. It's not contrived."

Bernard regards the Ryleys, Moores, and Voughts as ideal clients, because he was given the latitude to do what he believed in. He calls the enclosed garden at the Voughts an oasis, but it is, nevertheless, in sympathy with the natural environment and its limitations. At the Moores' and the Ryleys', he reached out and embraced the wild countryside. "What I've found in all my work is that, when you have a great native landscape, it's interesting just to amplify that."

All the buildings on the property, including this studio, were painted a color to blend easily with the landscape.

NANCY GOSLEE POWER

Mediterranean Courtyard

"Everything here is behind walls," garden designer Nancy Power says of gardens along the coast of Southern California. "When it's in the flats (rather than on hilltops), you tend to enclose. It's a Mediterranean way." Nancy's own cottage on a residential side street in downtown Santa Monica is a case in point. From the street, little is revealed; the white facade of the small stucco bungalow perched above a slope of agaves and aloes looks much like its neighbors'. But at the top of the steep rosemary-edged steps and beyond the door into the walled interior is a tiny, playful, Mediterranean-inspired paradise of color and pattern.

The property is minuscule, barely fifty feet wide and one hundred and fifty feet long, and most of it is taken up by two small houses. Nancy made two intimate courtyards paved with local California stone—the smaller one by the front entrance, and a more spacious one in back between the two structures. The front courtyard is shaded by palms and a red-flowered bottlebrush tree. Water splashes from a corner fountain in a painted yellow wall. A gnarled New Zealand Christmas tree (*Metrosideros excelsus* 'Aurea') leans picturesquely over a café table and chairs; terra-cotta pots of lilies and dahlias stand among iris, lavender, sage, and calendulas in a narrow border. Pots of succulents and geraniums are staged by the walls of the house, painted here golden yellow and white; the orange-tinged, yellow-flowering giant Burmese honeysuckle, *Lonicera hildebrandiana*, spills from the roof.

Two colors of California stone create a pattern in the paving of the tiny front terrace where a New Zealand Christmas tree is featured.

A narrow pebble path leads between the house and the boundary wall, also painted yellow and laced with jasmine, to the back courtyard. Here, between the two houses, on a terrace shaded

ABOVE: Nancy planted King palms, like pillars, to ground the back terrace, which is secluded behind colorful walls.

OPPOSITE: A white datura drips over the lily pool and spa. "When water is scarce, it becomes precious," Nancy says.

by palms and enclosed by walls painted vivid colors, surrounded by a bower of exotic foliage and flowers, Nancy celebrates outdoor living.

The place was completely derelict when Nancy bought it "at the bottom of the market" in the early 1990s. "It was considered 'a tear-down,' two little cottages filled with junk and the most horrible cat smells," Nancy recalls. But the two separate houses on a narrow city lot appealed to her—recently divorced, she needed a place not only for herself but for her teenage son, Oliver. "We called the back house the 'garçonnière' because he was eighteen and needed some privacy." She fixed up his nest first, then tackled the bigger cottage, only to find "that the stucco was holding up the house. Termites almost leveled it." Nancy gutted the place and, with the help of Bill Nicholas, an architect on her design staff, built herself a simple masonry structure consisting of three high-ceilinged, light-flooded rooms—a living room, bedroom, and a kitchen/library. "I had just been in Brazil," Nancy says, "and I loved the colonial Portuguese architecture with its tall, traylike ceilings made with boards and painted with stripes. I could have gone in the direction of Irving Gill, the early California modernist, and made it a little Bauhaus, but I thought I might sell it after a few years and that it would sell faster if I made it charming."

Charming it is, drenched with color and sunlight, French doors and windows flung open in every room to views of the garden. The walls and

LEFT AND RIGHT: A pebble path leads along the cottage from the front entrance to the back terrace where Nancy has created comfortable areas for outdoor living.

woodwork inside and out are washed with luscious hues inspired by the centers of tropical fruits. "The key," Nancy says, "was to relate every room to the outside, even if the outside was only five feet deep." Because the house sits on a long, narrow lot, the boundary walls on its two long sides are almost within touching distance. But Nancy creates vignettes on those walls to see from inside. The side view from the kitchen, for instance, is through a window, painted a glossy brick red, to a pot of coral succulents sitting in a niche cut into the high, golden-yellow wall just a few feet away. The kitchen, which Nancy sponged a comforting melony orange,

opens onto the intimate back courtyard where color dazzles at every angle. Each wall surface is a different hue. Directly ahead, the greeny-taupe facade of Oliver's house sets off a long, shallow pool, divided in two, the back half a spa for bathing, the front full of waterlilies. A faded sapphire-blue backsplash is centered on the spouts of water spilling into the pool. The high boundary wall on the left is colored a Moroccan purple-blue (inspired by the Marjorelle Garden), on the right golden yellow. The house wall itself, which extends from the kitchen to surround an outdoor fireplace and create a roofed porch sheltering a comfortable sitting area, is face-powder

Nancy deliberately repeated her neighbor's street plantings "to make it all of a piece," clothing the hillside outside her cottage with rugged agaves, aloes, and rosemary. Tall species marigolds add bright color.

pink. Door frames and outdoor café chairs are glazed a rich pink-red (Nancy calls it "turkey red"); the shutters on the cottages are celery green. The cushions on the courtyard's banquettes and the porch's rattan chairs pick up the chartreuse, Moroccan blue, and yellow of the architecture. "Somehow," Nancy says, "when you have a little cottage, you treat it very differently than you do a grand house with distinguished architecture. It allows you to be more playful. It's more primitive when you use lots of color."

In all the gardens she designs, Nancy excels at staging foliage and flowers against colored walls. In her back courtyard, she planted four King palms "to ground the garden and take your eye up, like pillars." She introduced the five-foot *Dianella tasmanica* with swordlike leaves and brilliant blue berries, and tall, russet-green bananas, for a Rousseau-like tableau against the deep blue wall. A datura, dripping white trumpet flowers, arches over the pool. Against Oliver's house, the agapanthus 'Dark Cloud' grows to five feet. A tall clump of feathery bamboo fills the corner. Black-green cannas are clustered against the golden yellow wall under one of the palms ("they come back every year and bloom orange"). "Cannas and bananas are a bit vulgar, but they look right here," she says. Nancy enjoys having outsized plants in her garden. "It's really fun to mess up the scale in a small space." (When the bananas get too tall, she just cuts them down to three feet.) "The palms and bold foliage plants provide the set—I think of it as the theater—then I fill in with the smaller plants," she says. She uses flowers to echo her color palette and then plays with different patterns and textures of leaves. Native and Mediterranean ferns, which thrive in the shade of the palms, are planted with the bananas and add a voluptuous jungle air. Chartreuse- and

maroon-flowered hellebores and blue cranesbills carpet the ground under-neath. *Salvia guaranitica*, blooming eight months of the year, picks up the vivid blue. Lime-green-flowered *Nicotiana langsdorffii* seeds itself around the courtyard. The little silver-leaved geranium with tiny, dark burgundy flowers, *Pelargonium sidoides*, spills out onto the patio from beneath the palms. "I like geraniums," Nancy says. "They suit the house, and they're tough. I don't like to baby plants." Although plants from the similar climates of the Mediterranean, New Zealand, the Canary Islands, and South Africa thrive in Nancy's Zone 10 garden, other plants take too much fussing in the ocean air. "We're a mile from the sea in what was an old sand dune. We have a lot of damp and fog, and it comes in the spring just as the little darlings have new leaves, so this rules out a whole lot of plants like roses." And, because Nancy has a full-time job designing gardens for others, hers needs to be low on maintenance.

For seasonal interest and added color, Nancy simply adds pots of plants to the garden. In May, magenta-flowered geraniums are staged around the pool; pink- and purple-tinged succulents in terra-cotta pots

"There's no bad color. It's how you use it," Nancy says. She excels at playing with hues in garden walls, cushions, and plants. On her terrace, dark cannas come up every year to contrast with the yellow wall. The palm is underplanted with plum-flowered *Geranium sidoides,* which echoes the purple of the bench cushion.

The beautiful foliage of hellebores and the sapphire berries of the flax lily, *Dianella tasmanica*, are set off by a red lattice and brilliant blue wall in a corner of the terrace.

line the steps to the front door; foxgloves just coming into bloom, lilies, and delphiniums in blue and purple are tucked in among the foliage of ferns and bananas. "In the wintertime, I have narcissus, South African bulbs, and amaryllis in pots; in summer, dahlias." By frequently changing the pots, she keeps the tiny garden fresh and vibrant. The brilliantly colored walls, dressed with the richly hued foliage of palms, bananas, and ferns, serve as a garden in themselves, with the pool and fountain as the centerpiece.

The sound of water is important to Nancy. "It masks the city sounds, so that when you enter the front gate you are immediately taken somewhere else." She loves hearing the water splashing at night in the small front fountain by her bedroom window. "Whenever water is scarce, it becomes precious," she says. "It makes you feel cool. In California, we've always had a water problem. It's why I chose not to have any grass, but to have courtyards instead."

All Nancy's work is appropriately influenced by this Spanish-Persian tradition of enclosed patios and fountains, but updated, made more dramatic and more colorful. Trips to Morocco and Brazil, where she thrilled to Roberto Burle Marx's own home ("the most sensual of all his work that I've seen"), made a lasting impression on her and intensified her love of brilliant, bold strokes of color. She is also much influenced by Luis Barragán's mentor, Ferdinand Bac, the early twentieth-century architect and garden artist from the south of France who took traditional Moorish design and made it more contemporary by using stronger colors. "He was a quasi modernist and also a romantic," Nancy says of Bac, though she could be talking of herself.

French doors open onto garden vignettes created with potted plants. "I'm always changing pots," Nancy says. In a tiny garden, this is the key to seasonal surprises.

The warm, vibrant, romantic home, which reflects Nancy's spirit, is her haven. Eight years later, she's not ready to sell. "It's nice, and it's a very functional, flexible house." It is also a perfect tiny example of the California aesthetic, where outdoor living is an integral part of every day. Nancy knows how to meld the inside and out with color, with views of plants, with comfortable seating everywhere you turn, with the sound of water splashing and dappled shade. "An exceptional garden," she once said, "is appropriate to its place." Nancy's garden, based on Mediterranean traditions, is wonderfully suited to its setting. Her artistic eye, her flair with color and pattern, her sense of drama in a small enclosed space, make it exceptional.

Art and Nature in the Northwest

Gardeners in the Northwestern coastal states of Washington and Oregon have a very different environment, both physically and culturally, in which to practice their art than we do on the East Coast. The setting differs dramatically: this is the land of timber, of conifers in vast forests, rimmed by mountain ranges, often snow-covered. It is also a land with a remarkably temperate climate, reminiscent of England, where gardeners enjoy mild winters (frost rarely lingers in the ground) and soft rains much of the year (although summer can be dry and often sunnier than reputation has it). In the gentle Zone 8 climate a great variety of herbaceous and evergreen plants flourish. One consequence is a proliferation of sophisticated plant nurseries to tempt the gardener, nurseries specializing in everything from hellebores to magnolias to rhododendrons to dahlias.

Culturally, the Northwest is a young land, settled by pioneers in the nineteenth century seeking a better way of life. The spirit of adventure that brought people here originally is evident in their gardens today—a freedom in design, a can-do-whatever-strikes-my-fancy mentality that results in a creativity that is lighthearted and often daring. Artwork abounds, from sophisticated to playful, in sculptures, fountains, ceramic, and twig work. It is a land of self-made dedicated gardeners and artists who are proud of where they live and the possibilities it offers; they are inspired by the freedom of their setting.

The two women profiled in the following pages are not exceptions. They are both passionate about the place where they live—on the dramatic cliff-lined shores of Puget Sound outside of Seattle, Washington. They are both artists, one a nationally prominent sculptor, the other a painter of colors and textures using plants as her medium. Their gardens are richly personal and celebrate their sites.

A native madrone, silhouetted on a bluff above Hood Canal in coastal Washington, is cherished for its colorful changing bark—cinnamon red in summer peeling away to lime green.

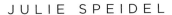

Sculpture in the Landscape

THE FAVORED OUTDOOR GALLERY FOR sculptor Julie Speidel's heralded bronze and limestone totems and figures is the garden she has carved around her home on Vashon Island. Its quiet drama inspires awe. It is a cathedral-like space, dominated by giant Douglas firs that filter the sunlight through their towering trunks onto pools of lawn. Curving beds of rhododendrons and ferns embrace the lawn areas, making them private and concealing one open area from another. Through the columns of trees, a verdant lawn flows past the low, dark-stained cottages that are Julie's home to a dazzling light of water just beyond—the property tumbles down a soft cliff to a deep, winding channel off Puget Sound called Colvos Passage. A certain reverence is felt in this garden, a sense of power and calm and simplicity, as the vertical thrust of soaring firs plays against the serene plane of green, lit beyond by the sweep of sea. Into this strong landscape, Julie sets her carved stones, figures, and totems. They stand silently in its shadows, echoing the lines of the trees, looking out to sea, framing the water view.

Seattle abounds with water views—glimpses of water are everywhere as the land fingers its way around the inlets and coves of the island-dotted Puget Sound. On a clear day the snowcapped Mount Rainier, as if in a Chinese painting, rises like a mirage above the Cascade Range of mountains that frame the eastern shoreline. Once inland, whether on one of the islands or the mainland, stands of majestic Douglas firs are the dominant trees of the place. For Julie, this extraordinary landscape of firs and sea is part of her childhood.

The four-acre piece of property on Vashon Island, where Julie and her husband, law

Three figures of sandstone and encaustic, sculpted by artist Julie Speidel, animate her garden on Vashon Island's Colvos Passage.

ART AND NATURE IN THE NORTHWEST

professor Joe Henke, now live was first discovered by her grandfather and father in the late 1920s. They had traveled over from Seattle on one of the small boats called the Mosquito Fleet that docked on land along Colvos Passage. From there they took a rowboat to explore the steep, salal-covered coastline of the island and found the piece of land where Julie's grandfather would build a house, and beside it a beach cottage for Julie's father, beneath great stands of fir trees. In 1975, Julie acquired that cottage from her father and settled there with her four young children. Twelve years ago, she bought the beach cottage and property adjacent to her father's place. This is where she and Joe now live, in simple spacious rooms lined with windows that frame the stunning seascape. Her father's house, now gutted and rebuilt, with a broad deck looking past the Douglas firs to the water, is reserved for visiting children, grandchildren, and guests.

At first the two lots were divided into rectilinear parcels, with a straight driveway in between. In the process of creating a garden, Julie's

OPPOSITE: A slab of ocean pearl stone placed on bronze feet by Julie serves as a bench beneath towering Douglas firs.

LEFT AND RIGHT: The curving pattern of tidal coves visible from the deck of the guest cottage inspired her contouring of lawn areas and grouping of shrubs.

A simple picnic table and bench is used for dining outside the guest cottage. Mature rhododendrons and native wax myrtles being cleared from a site nearby were rescued and planted four years ago to screen the driveway.

goal was to connect the two cottages by erasing what she felt were the unnaturally rigid lines of the property, "the rectangularity that society imposes on us." She wanted the contours of the land to flow, restoring the natural topography of the forest, as well as suggesting the curves of the shoreline below. First, Julie diverted the driveway, curving it in gently through the natural woodland of firs and maples and ferns, deliberately left wild, allowing merely a glimpse of lawn on the approach to the house. A second road branches gently off past a beautiful old katsura tree to the children's house. Then she and Joe boldly, fearlessly, cleared some of the great firs near the cottages in order to let sunlight in and allow for generous open areas of lawn. "It was very dark," Julie recalls. It is such a hard thing to do—to cut down great old trees in order for others to breathe. But Julie, the artist, knew that "there's this balance" between light and dark.

With the help of their gardener, Rod Ciceri, Julie and Joe brought in mature rhododendrons and wax myrtles to define the areas of lawn, and at times to shield one area from another. "I loved the Japanese way of closing and opening a vista to create surprise, light and shadow," Julie says. Joe, too, was influenced by this type of landscape, having grown up just north of Seattle in the Highlands in a garden designed by the firm of Frederick Law Olmsted, where generous sweeps of lawn were contained and hidden from each other by banks of rhododendrons and trees. Julie carved the lawn areas into amorphous shapes, with curving beds of shrubs and ferns, expanding and contracting. It echoes, Julie notes, the ebb and flow of the tide. She was especially inspired by the watery coves and inlets that surround the green-tinged, seaweed-littered, bird-inhabited, mud flats that stretch out into Colvos Passage for a quarter of a mile at low tide. "The land," she says with satisfaction, "now follows the sense of the beach when the tide is out."

Julie confesses to a love of flowers, which, she is certain, she inherits from her Norwegian grandmother who gardened in the Highlands district just north of Seattle, and was one of the founders of the Seattle Arboretum. But Julie knows instinctively that, here, she ought not to busy up (and thus destroy) the serenity and simplicity of her garden. Simple borders of flowers—annuals and perennials that attract butterflies and hummingbirds—are clustered against the cottages, but purposely kept to the side and behind, away from the water view. She is more excited about replanting native plants, restoring the natural habitat of forest and ravine on her four acres. Cedars once dominated this part of the island as well as firs, but they were logged by early settlers. Their great virgin stumps remain on the property, natural sculptures revered by Julie, decaying monoliths that

"I'm enamored of the beauty of rounded geometric shapes," Julie says of her circular bronze sculptures.

In curving her garden spaces to reflect the topography of the site, Julie feels she was "getting rid of the rectangularity society imposes on us."

speak of another time. Last year, Julie planted ten new cedars. "We won't know them in my lifetime," she realizes.

Vashon Island is remarkably carved by ridges, creating ravines and gullies that carry streams down to Puget Sound. This, Julie says, is what makes the island so wild. She and Joe are proud of the ravine that crosses their driveway. They have restored its edges with native huckleberry and bracken ferns, and cleared it of debris so that its stream once again runs free to the beach. Abundant ground water, which is evident in the numerous ponds and streams on the island, allows for liberal watering of lawn and newly planted shrubs and trees. It also keeps the island from changing much—water issues and the problems of septic systems keep building at bay. "The island is the way it was when I was a child," Julie says.

Having restored the natural topography of her land and established its air of serenity and theater with trees and lawn, Julie placed her evocative sculptures within this setting. Three sandstone figures, burnished red with an encaustic finish, stand quietly beside the Douglas firs, looking out to the water. A rounded geometric shape carved in bronze is set on a bench at the edge of the cliff, enclosing its view. A totemic form is placed by steps going down to the beach. A great slab of ocean pearl stone rests on bronze feet providing a place to sit in the shade of the firs and gaze

across the lawn to the sea. "As a sculptor," Julie says, "I think three-dimensionally. Form and shape are the cornerstones of my visual vocabulary and are drawn from the organic—the natural world—and from the human impulse to echo nature through the human mark." Northwestern totems as well as megaliths from ancient sites around the world influence Julie's work deeply. "Back then, they were saying: 'I was here. Take note.'"

And so, too, Julie is here, making her mark, in Seattle, on Vashon Island. She is of the place, an artist adapting to the land she loves for its innate beauty. Caring for her landscape and placing her sculptures within it strengthen its beauty. "There's an honoring you have to do to the land."

Simple borders of flowers that attract birds and butterflies hug the perimeter of the cottages.

NANCY HECKLER

A Colorist's Garden

Nᴀɴᴄʏ Hᴇᴄᴋʟᴇʀ, ʟɪᴋᴇ Jᴜʟɪᴇ Sᴘᴇɪᴅᴇʟ, lives under the spell of ancient Douglas firs on a property that is lit by water—six and one-half acres of wood, field, and orchard set high on a bluff above Puget Sound. Like Julie, Nancy is blessed with an artist's eye; her canvas is the land itself, her palette and paints are a catholic selection of plants gathered from two hemispheres. "We can grow anything here," Nancy says, referring to the gentle climate of the Pacific Northwest. Moreover, the availability of sophisticated plants from exceptional nurseries nearby is an enticement Nancy does not try to resist. Heronswood, for example, the specialist nursery famed for its cutting-edge offerings (some brought back from plant hunting expeditions in China and Japan) is merely fifteen minutes away. This ready supply of irresistible plants, of course, can be a danger-ous advantage, easily resulting in a mishmash of a garden, one that is of interest to collectors only, a display of specimens rather than a cohesive whole with a connection to its setting.

But Nancy's garden is more than a collection of exquisite plants. She combines her acquisitions with panache and places them in the landscape with sensitivity. Her goal always is to stay "true to the inherent character of the place." She integrates new plants with existing natives, and worries about the appropriateness of their placements, keeping her more exotic plantings near the house and choosing flora that is in keeping with the atmosphere of a farm for the orchard and field. Groupings specifically able to withstand sandy soil and wind are confined to the beach. "Great care," she says, "has been taken to maintain the rural character

Burgundy and dark purple foliage and flowers are a con-stant theme in this plant-filled garden above Puget Sound.

Nancy Heckler added plum-leaved *Rosa glauca* and clerodendrum to an existing stretch of white-flowering spirea for a lush mixed hedge along the entrance drive.

of the country farm with its rugged beach." Beyond this, she relies on her sure eye for stunningly rich, almost baroque, combinations of colors and textures to unify the garden, repeating a favorite color like a recurring melody, resulting in a floral composition of astonishing, painterly beauty.

Nancy and her husband, Terry, originally bought two and one third acres on Hood Canal, a spot called Oyster Point, in 1992. At the time, they were living and working in Seattle, where Terry has an advertising agency, but they were yearning for the country. "I wanted a farm," Nancy recalls. "I didn't really care about living on water, but my husband wanted water, and that combination was really hard to find without a huge amount of money." The small 1925 farmhouse that they discovered on this peninsula just north of Seattle sat on a carpet of lawn that ended with a bluff above oyster and clam beds. It had a view of water, the Olympic Mountains, and in the foreground, a statuesque one-hundred-fifty-year-old native madrone tree. Open farm land and an orchard, barely visible under a blanket of shrubby weeds, stretched from behind the house to a barn and a cluster of ancient Douglas firs. It was everything they both wanted.

Nancy quit her full-time job in marketing, and reverse commuted for a year and a half in order to oversee the clearing and renovation that needed to be done. A second story and a screened porch were added to the house without destroying its simplicity. The barn was restored, and they built a studio for Terry, who spends his free time painting. They were careful to echo the architecture of the old barn, then painted the studio the same traditional deep red as the barn and a nearby shed. Gradually, they cleared the orchard and adjacent field of Himalayan blackberries and Scotch broom. It was a painstakingly slow process, done by hand rather than with machinery in order to save the existing trees and shrubs; their reward was the uncovering of wonderful old fruit trees—plum, cherry, peach, apple ("one was a white apple")—as well as shad, lilacs, laburnum, and hawthorns that were part of the old farm plantings. Two years later, after they moved in, with the house renovated, the land cleared, the existing trees and shrubs ready for pruning, Nancy started her garden. She had gardened on weekends and after work in their city lot in downtown Seattle and accumulated a lot of botanical treasures. "I moved four hundred plants from Capitol Hill. It was still a war zone here, so I dug a little area near the house as a holding bed."

Nancy's first priority was to plant the north and south borders of the property to afford privacy. Great firs towered above the house and studio, the orchard and field protected them in back, and the water in front, but plantings were needed to block views of the neighboring houses on either side. Nancy brought in a "tapestry of evergreens" for screening, using

The Hecklers carefully restored the orchard they found engulfed with Himalayan blackberries and Scotch broom. Old orchards of apples, pears, and plums are a common sight in the region.

ABOVE: Tree peonies, epimediums, and hellebores—three of Nancy's favorite plant families—grow in the dappled shade of the Douglas fir woodland.

OPPOSITE: Artist Sue Skelly fashioned an arbor of Western red cedar and odd pieces of salvaged iron in the vegetable garden where fennel seeds itself with abandon.

conifers like the native shore pine, black pine, and cypress, and evergreen shrubs such as ceanothus and escallonias, which thrive in this climate. She extended the wooded areas by planting small-growing maples prized for their bark, like *Acer griseum* and *Acer davidii*, and magnolias of exceptional beauty. Then she filled in with cultivars of shrubs appropriate to her acid soil, such as witch hazels, rhododendrons, and hydrangeas. "I wanted to move the woods to the house," Nancy says. Today, the neighbors are invisible. North and south of the house, narrow meandering paths lead beneath evergreen and deciduous trees along shadowy ground richly planted with an eclectic but harmonious mixture of exotics and natives: tree ferns with a carpet of hellebores and lungwort, sword-leaved phormiums,

ART AND NATURE IN THE NORTHWEST

Any color goes with barn red, Nancy says of her husband Terry's new art studio, painted the same hue as the other outbuildings. Species dahlias, fennel, *Helianthus* 'Lemon Queen', and a chartreuse-leafed Japanese maple are staged in pots on the deck.

fine-foliaged, red-stemmed tree peonies, delicate epimediums, purple-leaved cow parsley (*Anthriscus sylvestris* 'Ravenswing'), white-flowering cyclamen. On the sunlit edges of the paths, tall Asiatic lilies nod overhead, euphorbias tumble at your feet, and everywhere, dahlias bloom in brilliant autumnal hues. Every path is an adventure, as one arresting still life succeeds another. What ties all these vignettes together is a constant thread of color, a repetition of the same shadowy hues—plums, dark crimsons, inky purples—in flowers and foliage. "I love any black flowers or dark flowers or dark foliage," Nancy says. 'Black Beauty' lilies, their reflexed petals the darkest burgundy, are repeated often along the paths. Ruby dahlias mingle with bronzy phormiums and purple-leaved smoke bush. Three varieties of dark-stemmed angelicas—*Angelica gigas, A. sylvestris purpurea,* and 'Vicar's Mead'—add their dusky, feathery notes throughout the garden. "You can't have too many angelicas," Nancy says. Against these deep notes, Nancy plays her brilliant reds ("I also love the color red"), as well as lighter hues. Choice, often unfamiliar plants delight the eye at each turn: spidery species dahlias in scarlet and copper, a lavender blue cranesbill with a white center (*Geranium* 'Buxton's Variety'), the small-flowered wild rose, *R. gentiliana,* with muddled white blooms, *Rhododendron sinogrande* with huge, glaucous leaves, silvery on their undersides. Certain plants are obsessions, namely tree peonies, dahlias, epimediums, hellebores, and roses.

The woodland gardens and intricately planted areas on the north and south sides of the farmhouse give way on the west to the simplicity of lawn and water beyond, with the great cinnamon-barked madroña on the edge of the bluff in solitary glory. Nancy has had the sense to leave the view alone. A path leads down from the bluff to the beach, edged in stone and planted with sturdy dry-loving plants like the native salal (*Gaultheria shallon*), which has decorative red stems and blueberry-like fruit ("the birds love it"). Hebes thrive here and the native ocean spray, *Holodiscus discolor,* in what Nancy calls her "built-in scree garden."

East of the house lies the orchard, preserved and honored by Nancy and Terry, heavy with fruit in September, garlanded with rambler roses in June. Beyond the orchard, bound by great firs and Terry's studio, is Nancy's most richly conceived artwork—her vegetable garden. It was the first garden she dug after screening her property edges. Forty yards of compost were incorporated into the sixty-by-sixty-foot bed to lighten the natural clay soil, after which Nancy sowed cover crops and tilled and

Pink and purple flowers are artfully mixed in a half-shaded sitting area near the house. Tall 'Black Beauty' lilies, plum-colored angelicas, and dahlias enhance a tapestry of appealing foliage.

Great clumps of orange and dark-red dahlias flower behind rows of purple-leaved kale and yellow-stemmed Swiss chard in Nancy's voluptuous vegetable garden.

tilled again over several years, trying to keep the blackberries from coming back. She divided the garden into rows running north to south, mounding them so that they warm up and dry out faster in the spring. Then she began planting her tapestry of vegetables and flowers. It is a serious vegetable garden with a thoughtful succession of peas and beans, cabbages, squash, corn and kale, chard and garlic and lettuces. But Nancy is interested in the beauty of the vegetables as well as their culinary use. Thus she grows many exotically marked and oddly colored varieties with expressive names, such as 'Oriole Orange' chard, 'Ruby Ball' and 'Red Jewel' cabbage, 'Tiger Cross' summer squash, and 'Flying Saucer' pattypan squash.

Along the rows, she adds bold brush strokes of floral color inspired by the vegetables— swaths of dahlias, amaranth, orach, and sunflowers. Certain plants, such as fennel and borage, are allowed to seed about giving the garden a lovely loose feeling, the entire composition an extravagance by late summer that is breathtaking. The huge shrublike stands of fennel thread throughout the garden. With its furry foliage and delicate wheels of chartreuse flowers, it gives the garden a soft feathery look that contrasts with a clump of bold-leaved bananas and the statuesque dahlias. Great clumps of tall dahlias, some with large shaggy heads, others with

tight pom-poms, ranging from the darkest black-red to brilliant scarlet or clear yellow, pick up the color of red-stemmed and yellow-stemmed Swiss chard, as well as a row of dark purple kale and another of maroon lettuces; these in turn are enhanced by the softer, duller red flower plumes of orach, *Atriplex hortensis.* Golden amaranth wave among sunflowers and dark-stemmed ornamental corn. Nasturtiums tumble over rows of cabbages. 'Tangerine Gem' marigolds ribbon a row of giant garlic. Although Nancy's palette runs from palest yellow to darkest red, including every imaginable color of green, a consistent thread of dark foliage and flowers binds the whole together, as in her other gardens.

It is appropriate to the place that dahlias are used as the floral stars throughout her garden, giving such grand punches of undiluted color, for they are wonderfully ubiquitous in this area of the Northwest. Every back road in Nancy's neighborhood seems to boast signs for "Pick Yr Own Dahlias," with glimpses in backyards of rows and rows of these late-summer show-stoppers. But here, in Nancy's garden at Oyster Point, they are used more artistically than I have seen anywhere else. Most of us plant a favorite tuber or two to thrust through perennials in our over-crowded beds or stand in a row in our cutting gardens. Nancy displays a great mass of each kind of dahlia, often as many as a hundred tubers in one clump (the dahlias don't have to be lifted in winter and have thus multiplied to this extravagant show over the years); then she contrasts the bold, brilliant flower heads with the soft, dull plumes of orach or amaranth.

Although Nancy's garden is her canvas, the result of her painterly aesthetic, she also enjoys collaborating with local artisans. The spiraling

Nancy combines her plants with an artist's eye, here playing golden yew, *Euphorbia stygiana, Senecio greyi, Geranium* 'Pink Spice', *Corokia cotoneaster,* and echeverias against the dramatic burgundy and pink-striped phormiums ('Dark Delight' and 'Jester') that she loves.

iron stakes that support her dahlias and lilies while seemingly dancing as they rise through the garden are the playful work of Lindsay Smith on nearby Bainbridge Island. "She's a plant person," Nancy says. She understands flowers. "I'll call her up and say I've got a *Rudbeckia* 'Herbstonne' that needs a support. She comes over, and bends the smooth iron bars to order." A ceramic artichoke placed under a prune plum tree in Nancy's orchard is the work of artists George Little and David Lewis whose well-known studio is also on Bainbridge Island. The artichoke contains the ashes of one of Nancy's beloved border collies along with a favorite Frisbee and a handful of pine cones.

Throughout the garden, Nancy encouraged her friend and neighbor Sue Skelly to apply her artistry. The fanciful arbors that add structure to her vegetable garden, the fence that weaves along the southern property line, the lattice on the shed wall—these are all structures imaginatively crafted by Sue from the inner bark of the Western red cedar. Sue has followed in the footsteps of the Northwestern Native Americans who used the native cedar in the same way. "It was their tree of life," Sue says. To make the arbors, she used cedar posts with pieces of salvaged iron that Nancy had accumulated. "I'm a metal junk collector," Nancy says. "I gave her all these metal pieces for the arbors and she put them together like tinker toys. She has such an imagination." Scarlet runner beans now climb one arbor roof made of old cavalry posts and woven cedar. Another arbor is fashioned from the frame of a Victorian cradle. Tall posts in the vegetable garden are topped with woven cedar balls, making perfect finials. By using the materials and the methods of the Northwestern Native Americans to make her cedar fantasies, Sue Skelly says she feels "connected to where I live."

Nancy, too, feels passionately connected to where she lives. She loves the traditions of the farm, the sea air, the forgiving climate, the infinite possibilities of growing plants. Best of all she loves "the anything-goes attitude" among gardeners in the Northwest. Experimentation, she says, is the key to an interesting garden. The lavish boldness and daring of Nancy's gardening style she thinks might result from her lack of horticultural training. She considers it liberating. "Sometimes people with training are so rigid," she says. "You can't do this, you can't do that. Well, why not? It helps not to have rules." She feels she has found her métier in life, making a garden. "This is the thing I was supposed to be doing. I'm lucky I can." Surveying her garden, Nancy says, "I think the house, the view, and the setting are all connected now." As indeed they are.

Euphorbia wulfenii 'Canyon Gold' billows beneath an arbor clad with white-flowering wisteria at the entrance of the 1925 farmhouse.

By Water's Edge

Gardening on the edge of the ocean has special problems as well as delights. The advantages, of course, are legion—cool nights, moist air, a gentle climate, often dazzling sunshine. But the destructive forces of wind and salt need to be taken into account, and the thinness of the sandy ground recognized. And very often there is a view—sometimes a vast panorama—that brooks no competition. One solution is to toss away the trowel and bask on the beach instead. But most of us want some designed landscape around our houses, if not beds of flowers. The biggest challenge, then, is to make a graceful transition between the garden proper and that powerful, natural expanse of water.

Both garden designer Edwina von Gal, at her beach house on Long Island, and the owners of Swan's Way in Nantucket, succeed in making that transition by subtly merging their gardens into the natural landscape and allowing nothing but large sweeps of natives by the water—the grasses and shrubs that naturally colonize in the sand and wind of the ocean's edge. No sculpture, no fussy flowers, no pattern of beds distract your eye as you stand in front of the view of dune, sea, and big sky.

The challenge of gardening on a property that features a pond is simpler—you don't have the same overpowering view—but the solution to making this smaller body of water seem comfortable in its setting is similar. How often we fail to make a new pond look settled on the land. How frequently it appears merely as a hole dug in a lawn sloping down from the house, a rowboat left upside down and forlorn on the grass edge. By planting the verges of the pond with colonies of native shrubs, flowers and grasses, and knitting the waterscape into the natural setting, as Edwina has done in one of the gardens in the following pages, you can achieve a sense of suitability.

The view of water is uncluttered from a cottage on Nantucket.
Simple bowls of white alyssum lead to a meadow rimmed with wild roses and bayberry.

Modernism on
Long Island's East End

"I THINK A LOT OF PEOPLE SHOULD BE forced to give up flowers for a while and create a landscape," garden designer and naturalist Edwina von Gal said one October day. She was standing in the garden she designed around the beach house she shared with her husband, Jay Chiat, on the eastern end of Long Island, looking at the shadows cast on the lawn by a gracefully twisting shad tree. "I love doing things with shadows," she said. "There's a lot in the landscape that people don't always see or think about—subliminal things like light and shadow."

Edwina has nothing against flowers. She recently made a kitchen garden for Ina Garten, the Barefoot Contessa of cookbook fame, which consumed Ina's entire backyard and was planted not just with vegetables but with masses of annuals in hues of orange and purple. And, at her own place here at the ocean, she has a tucked-away, fenced-in cutting garden chockablock full of blooms to bring into the house. She grows dahlias and "peonies, especially tree types, German iris in muddy colors, hardy lilies, particularly tiger types in dark oranges, herbs like horseradish and chives." She includes "kniphofias all orangey or lime, like *K. linearifolia* and 'Percy's Pride,' tender bulbs (tuberoses, callas, lots of acidantheras), alliums, tulips, hyacinths, nigellas, cornflowers, and yellow cosmos, which reseed, and orange 'Empress of India' nasturtiums." In 1997, she wrote a book appropriately titled *Fresh Cuts*, which captures the spare, often poetic arrangements she makes from flowers as well as the wild flora she finds full of beauty, like pokeweed and skunk cabbage.

The second-story deck of the beach house in Sagaponack provides a view over dunes planted with native bayberry, beach plums, and dune grass.

But a garden to Edwina is more about spaces and textures, trees and shrubs, light and

The barnlike beach house and arbor face the wild-planted dunes that are cut through with a path to the beach.

shadow. "People get distracted by flowers," she says. "They're just the pillows and ashtrays. People don't stop to think what's going to last, what makes a garden beautiful year round." Organizing and dividing space, contrasting textures, adding structure with trees, walls and paths, playing with water and light, and, above all, responding to the locale—these are the essentials of garden design to Edwina.

All these principles—and very few flowers—are evident in the landscape she created at her beach house in Sagaponack. Jay had commissioned the house before he and Edwina met. Architects Jane Sachs and Tom Hut of Hut/Sachs Studio were asked to design a modern structure from the frame of an old barn; Jay wanted the sense of space that a tall barn affords. Although the resulting house is small, it is wonderfully generous feeling inside—the kitchen, dining, and living are all in one room, with white walls to the beamed rafters and great expanses of windows framing views on the east, south, and west sides. The house was being framed when Edwina was recommended to Jay and hired to design a modernist garden around it. (By the end of the project, the two were married.)

The setting is a windswept, open stretch of land and beach on the edge of the ocean. A continuous rolling line of sand dunes runs across the front of the property, seventy-five feet out from the house, shielding the

sea from view. The vast horizontal plane of blue water on the other side of
the dune is only visible from the second story of the house and its bedroom deck. From the ground there is only the smell of salt in the air and
the wide empty sky and the sound of surf.

When Edwina arrived on the site, the dune was covered in poison
ivy—native and beautiful in its brilliant fall color, but a threat to bare legs
and bare feet, and invisible in winter. She quickly replaced it with swaths
of the native dune grass, *Ammophila breviligulata,* clumps of beach plums,
and colonies of scented sand-loving bayberry, which, with its rounded
shape and shiny deep-green leaves that turn luggage-brown in winter, is
handsome year round. A narrow path now cuts through the grasses and
shrubbery, up and over the dune, and down wooden steps past two weathered wooden chairs to the beach.

Grading the land between the house and the beach and establishing a
foreground of lawn to contrast with the wild shrubby dunes was her next

Edwina sculpted the rolling
lawn to make it roll and
undulate, then punctuated it
with shadblow, *Amelanchier
canadensis,* one of the island's
most picturesque native trees.

challenge. The soil in this part of Long Island is surprisingly rich—a four-to-eight-inch layer of clay loam dumped from a glacier on top of the existing sand. Bob Dash, who gardens at the celebrated Madoo nearby, compares the soil to chocolate cake. And like a cake, it is delicate. If you drive on it during construction (which, of course, is inevitable), you ruin it. And although it is tempting to add sand in order to lighten clay soil, that is a recipe for disaster, turning it into cement. Edwina tackled the compacted soil of the construction site, first grading it, then seeding it with the native red fescue, *Festuca rubra.* She laced the lawn with worms to help lighten the damaged soil and now yearly aerates it, popping out plugs of grass, removing them, then raking in organic matter such as dehydrated manure. The lawn that she made is not flat. It is mounded and swirled like a wave rolling in from the dune. In berming the lawn up in front of the dune, she disguised the "not very pretty bottoms of the dune grasses," solving what can appear an awkward transition between lawn and wild grass.

The harsh seaside conditions easily limited the selection of plants. On the wavy lawn in front of the dune, Edwina placed clumps of native shad, wriggly stemmed from the wind. Near the shad, she carved a small round reflecting pool in the grass, and, to one side, built a simple wooden arbor that shades a table and chairs for dining. The close-cropped lawn continues around the kitchen side of the house to the front, or land side, where it is again planted with shad. Two mature specimens contrast nicely with the simple geometric architecture of the barnlike house. *Amelanchier canadensis* is known fondly as "the Montauk shad" out here on the eastern end of Long Island where it occurs naturally in picturesque colonies.

Custom-cast concrete steps to the front of the beach house are set in the lawn to suggest a boardwalk.

Older trees are often rescued from sites that are being developed and, like these, transplanted to new gardens.

When planting a landscape, Edwina, like all garden designers sensitive to budget restrictions, is more likely to use young specimens of trees and shrubs. Having finished a project, she often stands back, its mature image in her mind's eye, and says, "Wow. This is great." The trouble is, "I see what it will be like in ten years. The client, underwhelmed, sees what it is now." Edwina explains to her clients that a garden needs three years before "it takes possession." She calls it, "Sleep, Creep, Leap." The first year the garden is seemingly sleeping while it is creating roots. The second year, plants are creeping. By the third year, she invariably hears from her client that the garden is leaping.

One third of the two-and-one-half-acre property on which Jay built their beach house is beach and dune; the rest of the land was a meadow with no existing trees or shrubs. Edwina's goal was to give the property some structure with plantings, like the shad trees, that would connect with the ocean setting. The grove of autumn olives that she planted to shield the entrance to the beach house from the road might also have existed, for they seed around in meadows here by the ocean. The olives, *Elaeagnus umbellata,* are not ecologically correct, Edwina says—they are not native

A pot of beach grass stands on paving next to a garden faucet.

and sometimes spread aggressively—but they thrive on the seacoast and are very much the vernacular. She prunes them regularly (with the help of Bill Miller, local "aborist extraordinaire") to give them their sculptural shapes. A path leads from the drive through rough grass beneath the shadowy olive trees out onto the small stretch of sun-lit lawn to the entrance door. By moving from light to shadow and then again to light, you are privy to a sense of mystery and surprise. The walk from the olives to the front door consists of large custom-cast concrete steps set in the mowed grass to appear "like a boardwalk. I wanted it to be the beach thing," she says.

To one side of the grove of olives, on axis with the great glass doors that open—like garage doors—off the living room of the house, Edwina placed a lap pool, its length lying half in mown lawn, half in high meadow grass. Jay didn't want a pool, Edwina remembers, but she persuaded him that it was important as an ornament, an element of the design. Because you don't see the ocean from the ground floor, Edwina wanted to have other water features that would reflect light—namely, the small round pool on the sea side of the house and this long lap pool. She stripped the pool of its usual accoutrements—stairs, skimmers, diving board, tile water line, coping. A scupper at the far end of the pool allows the water to flow out, as well as any debris, into a netted catch basin; from there it is recirculated. The pool's edge—gunnite covered with marble dust—is simply surrounded by grass. The pool reflects the sky year round, for it is left full in winter and uncovered. "I skate on it," Edwina says.

Just beyond the pool, a sculpture by Maya Lin sits in the high grass, a glittering pyramid of pieces of glass. On the far side of the house, artist Meg Webster created a steel sculpture over which recirculated water flows

down in sheets. "The birds sit right on it with the water going over their feet," Edwina remarks. She and Jay, who died three years ago, shared a special love of birds. Outside the kitchen door near the arbor, they set up a bird feeding table the size of a coffee table. "It was Jay's favorite place. They're the flowers," Edwina says of the birds that frequent the feeder. The only other hints of flowers at the beach house (besides her cutting garden, which is hidden away in a field across the street) are the golden-rod that has crept into the dune plantings, and blue camassia and daffodils (early pale yellow and late poeticus varieties) that she planted in the meadow around the far end of the lap pool. Large pots are used as ornaments also, filled with sedums and beach grasses, and clustered into a still life against the sunny walls of the house.

Edwina's modernist garden is simple, unpretentious, and appropriate, and, at the same time, imaginative. She took a small space, and without straying from the seaside vernacular, made it more interesting with grading and water features, and by subtly dividing its space, often merely by changing textures, moving from lawn to wild grass.

A lap pool, devoid of stairs, skimmers, coping, and diving board, is set half in lawn, half in tall meadow on the land side of the house. A pyramid of glass shards by Maya Lin is seen through a grove of autumn olives.

BY WATER'S EDGE

At an eleven-acre garden she designed nearby, Edwina played with the same elements on a larger scale. The garden surrounds a newly built, modern, gray-weathered house on what was once a potato field. Here again, she played with the contrast of lawn with meadow, planted trees appropriate to the locale and featured water to give the landscape light and interest. The handsome farmlike house opens out onto lawn, which is framed by a low, dry-stacked stone wall. To the south, the wall divides the manicured lawn from a meadow of tall switch grass (*Panicum virgatum*), a powerful visual contrast with its mass of soft waving inflorescences that turn amber in autumn. An old gnarled clump of black cherry trees leans picturesquely over the wall, throwing shadows on the flat velvet turf. To the east of the house, the wall defines the end of the lawn and the beginning of a cherry orchard. The cherries are planted in a broken grid—a tree was left out here and there so it would look like an old working orchard. On the west side of the house, the ground slopes significantly and is terraced with two stone retaining walls. The lawn spills down past the walls to high grass and a large pond.

The pond, in this case, is Edwina's water feature, and the focus of the garden. It had already been built when she was hired to do the garden, but it was surrounded by sod, and its workings, the inlet and outlets, were painfully visible. Edwina disguised the pipes and grates with stepping stones, and planted the pond with native species of grasses—*Panicum virgatum, Juncus effusus,* the common rush, and *Scirpus cyperinus*—as well as indigenous perennials and shrubs, taking her cue to some extent from a wetland preserve adjacent to the property. With Edwina's plantings, the pond is perfectly at home in its setting. Forget-me-nots paint its edges blue

OPPOSITE: Edwina naturalized the verges of a newly made pond on a Long Island property with native grasses, iris, eupatorium, ironweed, and sweetspire (*Itea virginica*) that are as beautiful in fall as in spring and summer.

ABOVE: The gently sloping ground from the house to the water is sparingly terraced with stone.

LEFT: Dry-stacked stone walls divide different areas of the eleven-acre property. An orchard of cherry trees gives way to lawn on one side and a field of switch grass on the other.

RIGHT: Edwina enjoys contrasting closely mown areas of lawn with wilder stretches of uncut grass.

in spring. Blue flag iris (*Iris versicolor*) blooms among the grasses. In summer, Joe-Pye weed (*Eupatorium purpureum*) and ironweed (*Vernonia noveboracensis*) flower in mauve and purple. Our native sweetspire, *Itea virginica*, which naturalizes easily in wet areas, displays fragrant white spikes in summer, and turns brilliant red in the fall. For height, she planted swamp magnolias (*M. virginiana*) and the beautiful native tupelo, or pepperidge tree, *Nyssa sylvatica*, which also turns gorgeous colors in the autumn—orange to red to purple. "I love ponds," Edwina says. "You plant them and the whole thing comes alive—birds, dragonflies, frogs. It just happens."

The feathered field of switch grass, the strongly patterned cherry orchard, and the light-filled pond look right—they are strong elements, but they fit in quietly with the spare, farm-inspired house and its straightforward agrarian setting. The landscape, Edwina feels, is a bridge between the architecture and the place, the *genus loci.* "You're supposed to be the translator," she says. "Architecture is about the architect. Landscape design is not about the designer. You can't insert your ego in the context of a landscape. You can have a signature style but only if you're working in one distinct environment, because the environment has to dictate the design."

Edwina opened a design business in 1984. For a number of years she had a large staff of associates, which enabled her to offer maintenance as

well as design. In the last few years she has scaled back considerably, with one landscape architect on staff and another who helps her occasionally with drawings. Instead, she happily relies on a community of artists and designers for collaboration, finding this a more exciting, creative approach.

Edwina's garden projects take her far away from her home territory. She is working on a botanical park project in Panama City with Frank Gehry, learning the tropical flora there with the same enthusiasm she has for knowing the native plants of her Long Island seacoast. And in Tennessee, she is collaborating with architect and artist Maya Lin, designing a sustainable landscape at Haley Farm for the Children's Defense Fund. The goal there is to cut down on maintenance by finding natural solutions for the land, allowing areas of high grass, restoring habitats, involving the resident children (everyone will plant a tree), organizing a pruning workshop so people will come and prune in the old orchard. "The whole idea is for a project not to become dependent on me," Edwina says.

Edwina excels at clean, understated, relevant garden design. The challenge as a designer, she says, is "to bring an informed, imaginative sensibility" to a project without it looking difficult or forced. "I'm fine with people not noticing what I've done," she says. "It doesn't have to hit you over the head all at once."

LEFT: A mown path invites strollers through the meadow of native switch grass, *Panicum virgatum*, which is a visually powerful presence in this handsomely understated garden.

RIGHT: The switch-grass meadow comes right up to the edge of the pond.

Nantucket Island Ideal

It is a perfect Nantucket garden. All the elements are there: the unobstructed view of water framed by a stretch of seaside grasses, the silvery shingled house, the rambling roses, the boxwood hedges, the hydrangeas. And yet there is something different, something more than the right elements put together—a restraint in the design, a paring down, a perfecting of a traditional idiom.

The island is known for its picturesque gardens. Common are old-fashioned borders where foxgloves play counterpoint to peonies, potentillas, and catmint in yards enclosed by high privet hedges just inland from the sea. Cottage gardens nestle in hollows away from the ocean winds, with gravel paths where lady's mantle and sharp pink cranesbills tumble in front of spikes of soft yellow phlomis, and fragrant honeysuckles twine over arbors. Perennials and biennials as well as roses and vines obviously flourish in this cool sea air.

Other gardens are not sheltered but open and exposed, with panoramic views of the harbor or the ocean. In some of these, the plantings between the house and the seascape are mostly of native shrubs and groundcovers—beach plum, huckleberries, bayberries, sweet fern, and little blue stem. The naturalistic plantings seem to enhance the distant view rather than compete with it. But often in these seaside gardens, the eye is distracted from the vista, disturbed by beds of colorful flowers and shrubs in the foreground. The flowers, no matter how pretty, seem busy in front of the scenic water; they fuss-up the view.

This is the challenge of designing a garden at a seaside property or, for that matter, on a

A low stone wall divides the arc of lawn from the natural landscape and water. The rambler 'Kiftsgate' climbs the roof of the cottage.

Opposite the serene water view is the garden's most glorious feature—old-fashioned climber and rambler roses romping up the walls and billowing over the roofs.

hilltop. There is not only the problem of coping with inevitable wind, but the difficulty of celebrating a view and at the same time having a flower garden. Russell Page's sage words in his seminal book, *The Education of a Gardener* come to mind: "If I were to choose a site for a garden for myself, I would prefer a hollow to a hilltop. A panorama and a garden seen together distract from each other. One's interest is torn between the garden pattern with its shapes and colours in the foreground and the excitement of the distant view. Everything is there at once and one has no desire to wander—to make discoveries." But if you have a view and yet long for a flower garden, he suggests placing the flowers "close against the house or below a terrace wall and so only visible when you turn your back to the view. I would arrange the gardened part of the garden—flowers and shrubs—to the sides or far enough below, so that they and the view are not seen at the same time."

The owner of Swan's Way seemed to know instinctively this wisdom when she made her garden. Just outside the house, a simple horizontal

stretch of lawn, bounded by a low curving stone wall, leads to a soft sweep of grassland meadow, bayberries, and the native rose, *R. virginiana*, beyond which lies the water. The uncluttered view is a serene panorama of liquid blue—first of a freshwater pond, then, past a sliver of sand dunes, the sea. But, with your back to the view, just a few steps out from the house, you see roses, masses of rambling roses in the softest hues of blush, cream, and yellow climbing the house walls, framing the windows, scrambling across the roof. Fat bushes of mophead hydrangeas cluster against the house and are hemmed in by low-clipped boxwood hedges. A bold geometric pattern of stones and grass define the terrace.

On the land side of the house where visitors approach Swan's Way, an oyster-shell path leads down through a lush screen of trees and high-growing privet from the driveway to the front entrance. Here, extending out from a broad porch, the simplest interpretation of a cottage garden is revealed. White painted arbors are covered with the climbing rose 'New

A linear pattern of stone and grass simply defines a terrace area next to the porch. Beyond lies the lush, wild Nantucket landscape of bayberries, huckleberry, sweet fern, and beach plum.

The old blush-pink climber 'Dr. W. Van Fleet' (parent of the less rampant, repeat-blooming 'New Dawn') is trained up lattice on the land side of the house.

Dawn' beckoning to a plain square of lawn enclosed by a picket fence and divided in half by a brick path leading to the porch and entrance. Within the enclosure, and against the white fence, a narrow continuous bed of fragrant white summer phlox edged in boxwood surrounds the lawn. That's all.

It is this restraint, this simplicity of detail that is so striking. Not only does the owner refrain from fiddling with the sea view, just lightly framing it with stone walls and lawn, with meadow flora beyond, but she has fashioned the surrounding garden to be astonishingly, serenely chaste. Squares of terracing or of lawn are bordered merely by narrow box-edged beds massed with one sort of plant. The varieties of plants she uses throughout the garden are limited to a handful, in a quietly consistent palette of colors.

It is not an old garden. The house, light-filled and exquisitely comfortable, was built fifteen years ago in the vernacular style with the help of architect Gwen Thorsen. Its shingled roofs are steeply pitched in the tradition of Nantucket, the walls gray shingle and covered with lattice, the windows plentiful, trimmed in white. The house is sited snug and low on the land, not perched high above it; rather than decks, porches and broad terraces extend out from the doors, making the transitions graceful from inside to out, connecting the house to the garden and the view.

At first, before the garden was established, there were no trees or shrubs to soften the new structure, which, according to its owners, looked as awkward as a cereal box. Trees were planted on the land side of the property to shield the house from neighbors and give it a settled look. Every year a few more trees were added, "a mixed bag" of native oaks, beech, and red cedars, wild cherry, Russian olives, dogwoods, and a specimen stewartia. An understory of native shrubs and groundcovers was left to spread undisturbed.

Originally the front garden within the picket fence contained a herbaceous border. "That," says the owner, who was born in England, the land of herbaceous borders, "was a disaster. The deer ate everything." And it was high maintenance. "So I decided to have just one thing that did well." The border was planted with *Phlox paniculata* 'David', the new cultivar of white-flowering summer phlox that blooms lustily and seems impervious to mildew. An occasional spraying with Bobex keeps the deer at bay. "It is a dream," she says. The fragrant heads of flowers last a long time, and, by cutting the stalks back after the first flush of bloom in late July, the phlox is encouraged to rebloom into fall.

Hydrangea macrophylla 'Nikko Blue' ("a seaside staple") clustered behind a low-clipped hedge of box is repeated in a border around the house.

Just as the front garden has been simplified over the years, so the little kitchen garden has undergone change. "I had a huge wooden plant stand from France there with lots of pots of flowers, and then the wind would come and they'd fall over. So I decided just to have green." White and green, that is. Standard 'Iceberg' roses and sweet-smelling jasmines bloom in large terra-cotta pots that are too heavy to tip over. Boxwood edges the small grass and stone terrace and a high privet hedge screens the neighbor's property. On the opposite side of the house, the path from front

Pots of roses and a painted bench decorate the entrance porch.

garden to back passes by a long narrow border, edged as always with boxwood. This bed holds nothing but a billowing block of Siberian catmint (*Nepeta sibirica*), its soft lavender racemes rising effectively above the trim green hedge. Here, too, a streamlining has occurred. Wanting bouquets indoors, the owner at first planted roses here for cutting; but the deer consistently ate the buds just as they were about to open. Out went the hybrid tea roses. The catmint blooms all summer and the deer don't like it.

The roses that climb the house walls and roof, however, are this gardener's pride and joy. Too high for the deer to dine on, the ramblers and climbers thrive in the sea air and sun. They are mostly old well-loved sorts, like the gorgeous buff-apricot Tea 'Gloire de Dijon', her favorite, which is covered with large fragrant quartered blooms and the Noisette, 'Madame Alfred Carrière', which does surprisingly well on this northern island, reaching the second-story bedroom balcony and heading for the roof. The Madame's loosely double blush white flowers are also highly fragrant and bloom continuously. The vigorous rambler 'Kiftsgate' covers the roofs with extravagant trusses of single white flowers in July. Masses of red hips follow in autumn. The rampant old blush climber 'Dr. W. Van Fleet', the once-blooming father of 'New Dawn', clothes the roof above the front garden. All the roses are tied closely to cedar lattices, and pruned hard after they bloom. Nowhere does a rose-covered cottage such as this—something most of us just dream of—seem more appropriate than on the Massachusetts shore of the Atlantic.

Beyond the garden and the shelter of trees, little was done besides clearing the foreground of the view of invasive vines and overgrown

shrubbery. The owner has since added wild ox-eye daisies to the grasses in what she calls her minifield, and clumps of the wild indigenous iris, and some pheasant's eye narcissus for spring pleasure. The meadow, bounded by bayberry and the wild Virginia rose, leads the eye softly and naturally to the far panorama of sea.

At first glance this garden seems predictable, it is so perfectly of the place—a lovely traditional Nantucket garden. And then its quietness reveals itself, its spareness, the understatement in its design, its refinement. Looking at this garden is like watching a skater or an artist who performs with such skill that what he achieves looks easy. But any experienced landscape designer knows that restraint is the hardest thing to achieve in a garden.

A porch on the land side serves as the main entrance to the house. Rose arbors lead to a small fenced-in garden of white summer phlox edged in boxwood.

ACKNOWLEDGMENTS

Warm thanks are due the garden owners and designers profiled in these pages for the time they gave me, generously sharing their homes, their views, and visions. I also wish to thank the friends who helped me develop the book, among them: Elisabeth Bishop, Diane Botnick, Michael Brennan, Susan Burke, Kim Dickey, Gregg Lowery, Sylvia and Ross Matlock, Mary McConnell, Patti McGee, and Dick Turner. I am indebted to Leslie Stoker and Janis Donnaud for their faith in me, and to my editor Jennie McGregor Bernard, who expertly and affectionately cleaned and polished my often bumpy written thoughts. To John Hall I owe the beauty of this book; his evocative, luminous pictures speak of his twofold talent as an artist and a lover of gardens. Laura Lindgren carefully wove those pictures with my sentences to produce a clean and elegant design. I thank my friend Wayne Winterrowd for kindly contributing his words to a foreword. Finally, I dedicate these pages to Francis Bosco Schell, my in-house editor and partner in every endeavor.

Published in 2005 by
Stewart, Tabori & Chang
115 West 18th Street
New York, NY 10011
www.abramsbooks.com

Canadian Distribution:
Canadian Manda Group
One Atlantic Avenue, Suite 105
Toronto, Ontario M6K 3E7
Canada

Library of Congress Cataloging-in-Publication Data
Dickey, Page.
  Gardens in the spirit of place / Page Dickey ;
photography by John M. Hall ; foreword by Wayne Winterrowd.
    p. cm.
  ISBN 1-58479-472-0
  1. Gardens. 2. Gardening. 3. Gardeners. I. Title.

SB455.D53 2005
712'.6—dc22   2005014543

Designed by Laura Lindgren

The text of this book was composed in
Original Garamond, Gotham, and Oneleigh Italic.

Printed in China
10 9 8 7 6 5 4 3 2 1

First Printing
Stewart, Tabori & Chang is a subsidiary of

LA MARTINIÈRE
GROUPE

PAGE 1: Iceland poppies bloom at Boone Hall in Charleston, South Carolina.

PAGES 2–3: The dry ground beneath a magnificent valley oak (*Quercus lobata*) in Los Altos Hills, California, is underplanted with drought-tolerant madrones and native bunch grasses.

PAGES 4 AND 5: Foxgloves, *Dianthus plumarius* 'Spring Beauty', and Tea roses are planted in profusion at Boone Hall.

07